The Sanctus Germanus Prophecies Volume 3

*Seeding the Mass Consciousness to Heal
Earth's Mental Body*

Michael P. Mau PhD

The Sanctus Germanus Foundation

Alberta, Canada

To purchase more copies of this work, please go to: **www.sanctusgermanusbooks.com** or **www.arberton.com**

Library and Archives Canada Cataloguing in Publication

Mau, Michael P.

The Sanctus Germanus Prophecies Volume 3: Seeding the Mass Consciousness to Heal Earth's Mental Body/ by Michael P. Mau. – 1st edition.

ISBN 978-0-9784835-1-7

1. Twenty-first century--Forecasts. 2. New Golden Age movement. 3. Finance 4. Economics

I. Sanctus Germanus Foundation.

Cover graphic "Dawning of the Soul on the conscious mind" by Matthew Thompson of the Sanctus Germanus Foundation

The Sanctus Germanus Foundation
Publications Division Alberta, Canada

www.SanctusGermanus.net

Table of Contents

PROLOGUE

In May, 2002 the Mahachohan of the Spiritual Hierarchy approved the release of information exposing the Dark Forces and how they operate in the world today. This information was first published under the title of *Beyond Armageddon* and two years later under the title of *The Sanctus Germanus Prophecies Volume 1.* Both publications seeded the mass consciousness with information about the Dark Forces which gradually took root among the thinkers of the world, not as another conspiratorial theory but as a logical explanation of the chain of events that would lead up to the 2007-2012 Global Financial Crisis. By 2012 this public exposure of the Dark Forces should be complete and everyone will know in one way or the other how they have come to control the world through their financial and warmongering systems.

Volume 2 Sanctus Germanus Prophecies followed and outlined a broad scenario of events that would overtake the earth during these times, in line with the waning of the current 26,000 year sidereal cycle. Both Volumes 1 and 2 continue to seed the mass consciousness.

We have now entered the most difficult part of the close- down of this cycle, as the Dark Forces ramp up their warmongering activities in order to survive. Mankind will experience the stress of a sinking world economy and may again acquiesce to the Dark Forces as they gin up another war to resolve the world economic depression. Choosing between another world conflagration and continued economic misery will constitute a major moral dilemma for humanity and determine how the Spiritual Hierarchy responds. Will the world today take the same a similar path that Atlantis chose?

Even though their low vibrational activities and institutions will inevitably crumble, the Dark Forces will not go down without a fight: a battle royal between light and darkness lies ahead. But it is clear that mankind has also chosen the more difficult path of suffering instead of rising up against the Dark Forces on all fronts. So be it. However long the cleansing may drag on, we can rejoice that the healing of earth's and mankind's mental bodies will be accomplished in the process.

To stack the deck on the side of light, a wave of lightbearers has incarnated on the earth during this time in order to balance the negativity that the Dark Forces have built up over the centuries. Many bring with them the expertise and talents needed to help humanity through these difficult times. However most are still asleep and the Spiritual Hierarchy can only hope that the stress of the times will eventually awaken them to take up the cross and fulfill their mission.

In this volume 3, we will project what we believe will take place in the next five decades. It is hoped that by about 2050 to 2060, earth will be well on her way to retrieving her balance after a major cleansing. We will offer some simple guidance to lightbearers and to an increasingly open-minded public about how to weather and navigate through this period of turmoil. We will draw from the Ancient Wisdom that has been laid forth for mankind to understand and use over the centuries and apply it to the current situation.

Taking this guidance to heart is an individual choice. We lay it before you in the spirit of offering you food-for-thought in a period of turmoil.

Chapter 1

Astral Plane Battle Manifests on the Earth

"What is apparent IS NOT, what is not apparent IS."

Sanctus Germanus

The battleground of the astral plane has now plainly manifested on the earth plane. Dark Force resistance has been strong yet mankind's reaction has been too lukewarm to prevail. All governments, including those democratically elected, have exposed their hidden mandates as proxies of the Dark Forces. Together and without shame they collude with one another to maintain their grip on humanity and suppress individual human rights to save themselves. This defiance of the cleansing cosmic forces has happened too many times during mankind's evolutionary journey, and the world's fate today is coming very close to repeating that of the sunken ancient civilisations of Lemuria and Atlantis.

Acceleration at Work

In *The Sanctus Germanus Prophecies, Volume 1* we signaled that our solar system had entered into the photon belt and would endure a long period of ever-increasing vibrations which we call acceleration. Scientific proof of this acceleration is elusive, yet everyone today feels it, primarily manifested in the rapid passage of time. By this inference we admit to being in the midst of acceleration, and as we observe our own societies, we can see that events are churning at a rapid pace, and all are experiencing upheaval in their lives.

Acceleration serves as a massive filtering and cleansing process that separates the good from the bad on ALL levels of human existence. Ready or not it is in force and ever increasing in speed. No one can escape it as it drives all those of lower vibrations insane. Newspaper headlines scream in shock at the atrocities individuals commit on one another. From regional wars to our quiet bedroom communities, insanity has taken hold.

Acceleration strips everything of any falsity or pretence and lays bare the Truth about ALL matters. Secret actions that do not serve humanity, from common citizens on the street to leaders at the highest levels of power, are exposed, sometimes in the most public and embarrassing manner. We witness bands of crooked politicians publicly apologizing for misdemeanours or gross crimes against their own constituents. Finance sector CEO's are being axed left and right as all who do not serve the interests of humanity are being summarily eliminated. Even Gurus peddling spiritual teachings in expensive high-powered seminars are being exposed. At home and among friends, those hiding behind false pretences and identities expose themselves by their actions. These times are just the beginning of the Age of Truth.

No Abatement to Acceleration

What we must understand is that there will be no abatement to ever-increasing acceleration for centuries to come. Acceleration guarantees the forward movement of mankind's evolution from the dense physical into lighter spiritual beings. No man, government, or organisation—even the Dark Forces-- can stop it. They might be able to slow down the forward momentum but they cannot stop the inevitable. If they succeed, more energy builds up behind the great dam of change to culminate in catastrophic events that force the advance of evolution by explosive actions. So looking nostalgically back to the "times past" and the return to what used to be is fruitless.

For those who yearn to see the dawn of the New Age, acceleration cannot move fast enough. And if they must sacrifice much so that this process could move faster, then they are willing to let go all they have and flow with the energies. Yet these are still outnumbered by those who cling to the icons and assets of the present civilization. But if they do not let go, then they cannot survive the closing of this present cycle. Those who flow with the changes, serving humanity as best they can, will survive.

The Cosmic Law of Periodicity: the Compelling Nature of Cycles

Acceleration coincides with the inevitable waning of a major cycle. All phenomena on earth and the Universe play out in cycles. From the second to the minute, hour, day, week, month, year, decade, century, millennia, aeons, manvantaras, yugas etc. we move in cycles. As we explained in Volume 2 of *The Sanctus Germanus Prophecies*, we are coming to the end of a 26,000 year cycle known as the earth's precession or Earth's Great Year. Neither mankind nor the Spiritual Hierarchy can alter this great waning cycle as it plays out under cosmic law.

All cycles wax and wane, and earth must cleanse all that do NOT serve mankind in order to prepare for the next great cycle. Within this final stage of Earth's Great Year, there are multiple mini-cycles, all of which take on the character of the great waning stage. They account for emotional ups and downs, the alternating pessimism and optimism in the populations, the volatility of the markets, and the general instability of all that have been taken for granted--all happening as the great overall cycle winds down.

Within each cycle lie several choices, the two main ones of which are 1) to flow with the cycle and allow the cleansing or 2) to fight the cycle and resist the cleansing. The latter is what earthlings are now doing.

Divine knowledge and wisdom would have the cycle end as soon as possible while the self-preservation instincts of mankind and the Dark Forces would have it drag on indefinitely. Such is not possible, for the cycle falls under the compelling Cosmic Law of Periodicity and must be brought to an end under cosmic time.

World Karmic Balancing at End-of-Cycle

A major balancing of world karma also coincides with the waning cycle and acceleration. Humanity, in general, has for centuries acquiesced to the Dark Forces domination on earth. It has succumbed readily to Dark Force propaganda with little resistance, a fraudulent money regime and taken part in warmongering like so many apathetic sheep. As a result, much negative karma has accumulated as violations of cosmic law continue every second of the day.

Sixty years following the end of World War II, the energies on earth remain cockeyed, listing heavily on the side of negativity. All sorts of heinous crimes against humanity, unimaginable theft through the invisible hand of manufactured inflation and the impoverishment of the masses through the mal-distribution of resources are just a few of the actions that have brought about this imbalance.

Most of all, almost every year since the official close of the World War II, some form of ongoing war-for-profit has taken place to keep their arms industry humming. Below is a list that shows the magnitude of the Dark Force warmongering activities and their fatalities since post-World War II, all of which have contributed to the great karmic imbalance on earth:

1946-49: Chinese civil war (1.2 million)
1946-49: Greek civil war (50,000)
1946-54: France-Vietnam war (600,000)
1947: Partition of India and Pakistan (1 million)
1947: Taiwan's uprising against the Kuomintang (30,000)
1948-1958: Colombian civil war (250,000)
1948-1973: Arab-Israeli wars (70,000)
1949-: Indian Muslims vs. Hindus (20,000)
1949-50: Mainland China vs. Tibet (1,200,000)
1950-53: Korean war (3 million)
1952-59: Kenya's Mau Mau insurrection (20,000)
1954-62: French-Algerian war (368,000)
1958-61: Mao's "Great Leap Forward" (38 million)
1960-90: South Africa vs. Africa National Congress (unknown number of deaths)
1960-96: Guatemala's civil war (200,000)
1961-98: Indonesia vs. West Papua/Irian (100,000)
1961-2003: Kurds vs. Iraq (180,000)
1962-75: Mozambique Frelimo vs. Portugal (unknown number of deaths)
1964-73: USA-Vietnam war (3 million)
1965: second India-Pakistan war over Kashmir
1965-66: Indonesian civil war (250,000)
1966-69: Mao's "Cultural Revolution" (11 million)
1966-: Colombia's civil war (31,000)
1967-70: Nigeria-Biafra civil war (800,000)
1968-80: Rhodesia's civil war (unknown number of deaths)
1969-: Philippines vs. New People's Army (40,000)
1969-79: Idi Amin, Uganda (300,000)
1969-02: IRA - Northern Ireland's civil war (2,000)

1969-79: Francisco Macias Nguema, Equatorial Guinea (50,000)

1971: Pakistan-Bangladesh civil war (500,000)

1972-: Philippines vs. Muslim separatists (Moro Islamic Liberation Front, etc) (120,000)

1972: Burundi's civil war (300,000)

1972-79: Rhodesia/Zimbabwe's civil war (30,000)

1974-91: Ethiopian civil war (1,000,000)

1975-78: Menghitsu, Ethiopia (1.5 million)

1975-79: Khmer Rouge, Cambodia (1.7 million)

1975-89: Boat people, Vietnam (250,000)

1975-90: civil war in Lebanon (40,000)

1975-87: Laos' civil war (184,000)

1975-2002: Angolan civil war (500,000)

1976-83: Argentina's military regime (20,000)

1976-93: Mozambique's civil war (900,000)

1976-98: Indonesia-East Timor civil war (600,000)

1976-2005: Indonesia-Aceh (GAM) civil war (12,000)

1977-92: El Salvador's civil war (75,000)

1979: Vietnam-China war (30,000)

1979-88: the Soviet Union invades Afghanistan (1.3 million)

1980-88: Iraq-Iran war (1 million)

1980-92: Sendero Luminoso - Peru's civil war (69,000)

1980-99: Kurds vs. Turkey (35,000)

1981-90: Nicaragua vs. Contras (60,000)

1982-90: Hissene Habre, Chad (40,000)

1983-: Sri Lanka's civil war (70,000)

1983-2002: Sudanese civil war (2 million)

1986-: Indian Kashmir's civil war (60,000)

1987-: Palestinian Intifada (4,500)

1988-2001: Afghanistan civil war (400,000)

1988-2004: Somalia's civil war (550,000)

1989-: Liberian civil war (220,000)

1989-: Uganda vs. Lord's Resistance Army (30,000)

1991: Gulf War - large coalition against Iraq to liberate Kuwait (85,000)

1991-97: Congo's civil war (800,000)

1991-2000: Sierra Leone's civil war (200,000)

1991-2009: Russia-Chechnya civil war (200,000)

1991-94: Armenia-Azerbaijan war (35,000)

1992-96: Tajikistan's civil war war (50,000)

1992-96: Yugoslavian wars (260,000)

1992-99: Algerian civil war (150,000)

1993-97: Congo Brazzaville's civil war (100,000)

1993-2005: Burundi's civil war (200,000)

1994: Rwanda's civil war (900,000)

1995-: Pakistani Sunnis vs. Shiites (1,300)

1995-: Maoist rebellion in Nepal (12,000)

1998-: Congo/Zaire's war - Rwanda and Uganda vs. Zimbabwe, Angola and Namibia (3.8 million)

1998-2000: Ethiopia-Eritrea war (75,000)

1999: Kosovo's liberation war - NATO vs. Serbia (2,000)

2001-: Afghanistan's liberation war - USA & UK vs. Taliban (40,000)

2002-: Cote d'Ivoire's civil war (1,000)

2003: Second Iraq-USA war - USA, UK and Australia vs. Saddam Hussein (14,000)

2003-: Sudan vs. JEM/Darfur (200,000)

2003-: Iraq's civil war (60,000)

2004-: Sudan vs. SPLM & Eritrea (unknown number of deaths)

2004-: Yemen vs. Shiite Muslims (unknown number of

deaths)

2004-: Thailand vs. Muslim separatists (3,700)

Arab-Israeli wars

I (1947-49): 6,373 Israeli and 15,000 Arabs

II (1956): 231 Israeli and 3,000 Egyptians

III (1967): 776 Israeli and 20,000 Arabs

IV (1973): 2,688 Israeli and 18,000 Arabs

Intifada I (1987-92): 170 Israelis and 1,000 Palestinians

Intifada II (2000-03): 700 Israelis and 2,000 Palestinians

Israel-Hamas war (2008): 1,300 Palestinians

Unless involved directly in any of these wars, most readers probably have little or no recollection of all these wars. The Dark Forces have learned to engineer these money-making wars so that they do not inconvenience the world's populations, yet the diversion of the earth's resources to the production of arms and military *materiel* has resulted in a mal-distribution of wealth on earth where masses live in poverty and a few live relatively comfortable lives. Peace movements, largely financed by the Dark Forces, have naturally failed to stop the Dark Forces from making war for profit. It is no wonder that after so many staged wars-for-profit involving millions of deaths, a karmic rebalancing is due equal to amount of apathy the world population has demonstrated. Who must pay for this karmic rebalancing? Humanity itself; hence the suffering that is to come as the Dark Forces exit the earth plane.

No Turning Back

As the cosmic timetable plays out, those who yearn for the good 'ole days or for things to go back to normal will be the first to be swept away as the turmoil increases. Those who flow with the changes and take appropriate action to adjust their lifestyles, even if it means uprooting themselves from a safe and comfortable life, will survive the convergence of these cosmic factors. For others who opt for no change, survival is not an issue; they can always reincarnate to continue their journey of evolution in another context. Whether we survive this transition or not, we will all end up at the same point of evolution one day, so how we act in the coming years of turmoil is purely a matter of choice.

Global Financial Playground

It is in the international arena that the Dark Forces play their hand without much public scrutiny; that is why Dark Force financiers seem to be disconnected from the rest of the planet . . . that is, until things begin to crumble and they need more money.

Ninety-nine point nine percent (99.9%) of the world's population does not realize that trillions of dollars circulate around the world per milli-second serving the interests of a small clique of financiers and government politicians. Sophisticated computer systems trade billions of shares per milli-second, swooping through the international financial markets and collecting profits from billions of milli-second transactions. This is how giant investment banks pocket billions in profit, while the world writhes in economic pain and billions go hungry daily.

Central banks of the world manipulate interest rates constantly, so on one side of the globe they are lower than on the other side. Money flows from low interest rate zones to higher rate zone, effortlessly making a profit on the interest rate difference without any public scrutiny. Hedge funds serving the interests of the Dark Force central banks and government agencies, act as proxies that play this interest rate game euphemistically called "the carry trade." The most lucrative has been the "Japan carry trade" where for more than a decade, investors borrowed at low interest rates in Japan to invest in higher interest bearing instruments in the US and Europe. Banks just move the money from one pocket to another, earning trillions without producing a single widget.

Like the hydra-headed dragon in the Bible, no sooner had this "carry trade" unravelled in 2007, than it popped up in other regions of the world. This time the US took over from Japan as a cheap source of money to be invested in other higher yielding countries. Again, these multi-billion dollar trades take place in an international financial wonderland while great suffering of the world's population takes place.

The enormous derivative market, both publicly and privately traded, is a major component of this financial playground. It is said that the large investment banks own ninety-four percent (94%) of the existing derivatives. Swollen to an aberrant sum of $750 TRILLION, the implosion of these derivatives will serve as the last nail in the Dark Forces' coffin. This is the swollen dragon referred to in the Book of Revelations that hangs over the earth today, and like humpty dumpy, it will fall off the wall and come tumbling down. When this monetary charade collapses, taking with it the world's paper currencies, mankind will re-discover that life will continue on the planet as if derivatives never existed, and mankind will adjust to the reinstitution of gold and silver as a means of monetary exchange.

Astral Quicksand Underlying the Financial System

The entire world economic and financial system is based on mankind's desires and wants. It is built out of astral and lower mental matter. Astral matter gives mankind's desires and wants form, while lower mental matter manifests as sophisticated computer and trading systems that the human brain has devised to enable a virtual stranglehold on the finances of this earth. It also manifests as the big bank towers and government buildings that give the impression of stability and solidity. Yet the underpinning of these impregnable financial fortresses is very shaky, built of astral wants, whims and desires. This is the astral foundation of quicksand upon which the Dark Force empire is built.

To feed this system, the Dark Forces have devised every means possible to stimulate emotions that would anchor mankind in a world of ever-increasing desire for material things. The craving to shop, especially to satisfy personal emotional voids, has driven the world for decades. This is euphemistically called "consumer spending". When these desires risked being dampened for lack of money, the Dark Forces refuelled the system with huge amounts of electronic credit that took the form of credit cards, home equity loans, car loans and consumer credit loans. Then when the consumer could no longer pay back the credit and interest, the system began to collapse. This is where we stand today. Where can it go from here? Our leaders prescribe more credit as the solution. But even massive amounts of electronic credit cannot stop a waning cosmic cycle!

Add to this, acceleration. It rumbles through the earth's astral plane and then into the etheric and physical planes. On the astral plane it causes commotion and emotional upheaval, which in turn sets off emotions such as fear, panic, complacency and insanity in our astral bodies. Humanity and its markets are whipsawed from one end of the emotional spectrum to the other, and the shaky astral foundations of the world's banking and financial systems begin to rock and eventually disintegrate. Despite the impregnable appearance of their buildings and infrastructure, the whole system sits on nothing but emotional quicksand that is being bombarded by acceleration. This is why this system of finance is destined to be sucked into the astral quicksand and topple.

The Scorched Earth Strategy

Treading in this quicksand of astral desire and wants, the Dark Forces are very aware that their financial playground is about to shut down. They, too, understand the nature of cycles and karma. Black magicians under their employ can also see the end of the sidereal cycle and how the incoming acceleration can roil their systems. These are undeniable cosmic facts. Thus, they have adopted the scorched earth strategy: if they go down they will drag all humanity down with them. Such a strategy portends a significant struggle which will result in much "collateral damage" to human society.

Dark Force scientists and black magicians claim they have the means to alter cosmic cycles and provoke or interfere with geological changes in the earth's structure. They claim to possess just as much power and know-how as the light forces of the Spiritual Hierarchy. This braggadocio remains to be borne out in action but it does show the high level of resistance to cosmic trends we can expect from them.

What they do control and manipulate are their own inventions: the world's stock markets, commodity exchanges, bond auction markets, and the private and public derivative markets. They also control the world's giant smokescreen, the mass media, which is like the control panel to earth's astral plane from where they manipulate the emotional bodies of the world's population.

Through the media, the Dark Forces control the psychological mood of the masses by painting optimistic pictures to trick private investors to invest more of their money in the markets. A few crumbs are thrown their way and more investors jump in. Once the money is in the market, the Dark Forces can reverse the direction of the markets and reap in huge sums through their contrarian investments.

The Dark Forces have designed the markets so that they profit when the markets go up and when they go down. When they see large numbers of investors betting on the markets going up, they slam the market in the downward direction and take the investors' money. By controlling both directions of the markets, they "win" either way. And through the chorus orchestrated in the mass media, they can get investors running in either direction. The Dark Forces will always take opposite positions to those of the world's investors to reap in the profits at their will. Even the most expert of technical and market analysts cannot accurately predict the whims of those who control the markets, for they are still under the delusion that free market forces are behind the financial markets. It's a game of psychological manipulation, where the Dark Forces have mastered how to use mankind's "herd instinct" for their own benefit.

As if thumbing their noses to the world suffering from the effects of an unprecedented economic depression, the agents of the Dark Forces, the large investment and commercial banks, continue to gouge the derivative markets for obscene profits. They have returned to the trough even after the crisis of 2007 to 2008. Now, flush with funds from their collusion with the governments, they continue to speculate in derivatives related to basic foods of the world's populations such as rice, wheat, soy, and corn, as if they existed in a financial wonderland of profits on another planet. They play with essential energy derivatives on the commodities markets in natural gas, petroleum and even alternative sources of energy as if completely detached from mankind, driving prices out of reach of the common person and causing untold hardships to the world's population. Their complete disregard for the social and economic consequences of their actions only reinforces our view that the Dark Forces are the throwbacks of un-evolved souls.

Cosmic trends portend the destruction of the Dark Forces. Their agents, the banking industry, know that the banking system is insolvent and unsalvageable. Like rats abandoning a sinking ship, the boards of directors, their CEO`s and high level management staff seek to milk every penny from the sinking ship. Outrageous executive bonuses are an indication of this exit policy. As their greed, panic and desperation increase, any semblance of basic morals, e.g. `Thou shalt not steal`, is erased from consciousness.

Like the errant Lucifer who in defiance of the Spiritual Hierarchy chose the path of darkness, the Dark Forces are still aware of the constant presence of the governing Spiritual Hierarchy looking down upon their acts. Yet in wholesale defiance to cosmic laws and the Spiritual Hierarchy's scrutiny, they proceed to carry out their scorched earth strategy. Humanity's acquiescence has emboldened them.

Each battle is played out in mini-cycles. After each crisis, the quicksand of panic, fear, wants and desires temporarily subsides until acceleration again roils the astral plane, sending panic throughout the markets. This is a test of endurance: on one side the Spiritual Hierarchy with boundless cosmic energy and on the other, the Dark Forces with their material forces and money. Eventually, energies of the higher forces will crack the Dark Force control of their markets as it gradually slips with each wave of acceleration. Until then they are not ready to give up. They have already planned what to do when the world is on its knees financially and economically and there is a threat of insurrection and revolution from the public.

The spread of government-fabricated diseases is already underway. The AID-HIV virus is an example. Other attempted pandemics such as the SARS panic have failed to materialize, and more draconian measures are planned. This time the Dark Force health agents and the media will ramp up scare tactics to panic the public into accepting mass vaccinations. By forcing vaccinations on a sheep-like population, the Dark Forces plan to *spread* rather than stop pandemics.

Each vaccine will be laden, not with the antidote to the targeted pandemic, but with more "incurable" diseases that can bloom into the actual pandemics they have been trying ignite. The vaccinated will serve as live disease carriers to infect the people with whom they come in contact. The imagination can only wonder at the havoc the ensuing pandemics will cause the world.

The goal is to reduce the population to manageable numbers. The runaway population explosion on earth during the past two centuries has made it almost impossible for the Dark Forces to bring the global population under their complete control.

Poverty-stricken, starving populations are much easier to control than affluent ones, so a pandemic in a poor country will not have the same effect as one in an affluent nation where opposition can easily arise from an educated public.

Dark Force Accumulation of Gold and Silver

Part of the Dark Force exit strategy consists of draining all existing pockets of wealth—government and private pension funds, trust funds, stocks and bonds, derivatives, private retirement accounts. Knowing that paper currencies and other paper financial instruments they have invented will soon be worthless, they have been purchasing huge amounts of gold, silver and precious metals with electronic or paper money. Through the derivative gold futures market, they have been able to hold the price of gold at artificially low prices to give paper money even more buying power. This is yet another clever trick of "getting something for nothing," *an alchemy that transforms worthless paper into gold.*

There are also reliable reports that the Dark Forces, in collusion with the governments, have been substituting the official reserves of pure gold bars (i.e. such as the store in Fort Knox) with "salted" gilded tungsten bars, a heist that will go down in history as the greatest theft. When revealed to the public, this scandal will undermine the foundations of the world's monetary system and lead to its collapse.

When this neat jig is up, and the Dark Forces have accumulated their mountainous stores of gold, the price of gold on the world market will soar beyond imaginable limits. This will be the signal that the Dark Forces have accumulated enough gold and silver to control the world.

Yet little do they know that gold bears intrinsic esoteric qualities such as purification, vitalization and rebalancing that will create havoc for them. The more gold they hoard, the more it will purify and rebalance the preponderant masculine energies they use to control the world. So from an occult perspective, gold will join the other factors of acceleration, cyclic ending and karma to undermine the Dark Forces.

Government Collusion with the Dark Forces

For their life support system, the Dark Forces can force democratically elected governments, oligarchies and dictatorships to transfer their respective countries' wealth from their countries to Dark Force coffers in Switzerland and other financial capitals. Termed government "bailouts", these transfers of enormous sums of money to the Dark Force coffers are cast as "saving the people" from a systemic financial meltdown. In reality it is a ruse to empty government coffers before confidence in electronic and paper money crumbles in order to convert phantom money into solid gold.

Governments must comply with the Dark Force demands, because all governments are heavily indebted to them. The Dark Forces hold government bonds and debt instruments through their agents and proxies, i.e. the banks and hedge funds. So as creditors, they can force any national government that is indebted to them to do whatever they please, the United Kingdom and the United States being the prime examples.

The global financial crisis has thus brought to the surface and to public attention the outright collusion between national governments and the Dark Forces. It is a collusion that has been going on for centuries, only under monarchs, dictators, emperors, oligarchies and warlords. The difference in today's world is that there is no effort to conceal the scale of the collusion, and government funds are blatantly passed through the international banks into the hands of the counting houses in Switzerland with a "take it or leave it" attitude.

Public protests against this collusion have fallen upon deaf ears, as legislative bodies ram through policies "for the good of the public". For example, the US Congress under pressure from the banks not only rammed through bank bailouts but also passed a law to change the accounting rules so that banks no longer had to value their assets according to the market but solely as they please. As a result, their toxic assets holdings suddenly took on fictitious values overnight, and insolvent banks suddenly declared themselves back in profit. They have managed to delude the public into thinking that the economy and financial system are on the mend. In reality financiers know the situation is hopeless and that it is a matter of time before the whole system collapses.

Government Bureaucracies Scramble to Survive

The survival of the international, national, and state/provincial governmental bureaucracies, which all ultimately depend on national tax revenues to exist, is now at stake. As government coffers empty, their bureaucracies will be left high and dry. Today, they are scrambling to save themselves from extinction by trying to convince a weary and broke public that their services are vital to save the people from the collapsing economy.

Even while homeless, suffering people live in tent camps outside state capitals, the bureaucracies think of their own survival first. They will draw up policies to raise taxes to preserve their salaries and fiefdoms. When the public rejects their tax increases, they will retaliate by exacting fees and commissions from the public for their services. Police and law enforcement brigades hide behind blind curves on the highways to trap speeders and increase the daily take on penalty revenues. They spend millions on high technology "enforcement" devices to monitor parking meters, enforce speed limits and pay support staff to administer the intake of increased revenues. In some countries, even if bureaucrats are not being paid, they will still sit at their desks and exert whatever power they have to milk the public with extraordinary fees, penalties, stamps, petty taxes on consumer items and commissions.

To sooth possible backlash from the public, bureaucracies pretend to work for the people by reducing staff and cutting expenses. In reality only low-level staff and contract workers get laid off, while the salaried and tenured hang on. These latter represent government bureaucrats who by virtue of the time they put in "in service" hope to survive so they can live on their government retirement pensions.

However, for the past decade, the Dark Forces have targeted both government and private pension funds and in the end will succeed in draining them of all their worth, since the funds have invested in stocks and bonds in markets that the Dark Forces own. Furthermore, as these pension funds begin to teeter on insolvency, the very government agencies and private insurers that are supposed to guarantee these funds from insolvency will also be found to be effectively bankrupt. Leaving retirees high and dry is part of "the collateral damage" the Dark Forces plan to inflict on the populations around the world as they exit.

Those targeted for mass vaccinations are institutional workers such as government bureaucrats and large corporation employees that would be associated with these large pools of pension money. They constitute an educated sector of society that must be quelled before the Dark Forces can proceed with further extraction of value from their pension funds.

So as tax revenues diminish in the economic depression and the Dark Forces drain the people's retirement pensions, impoverished, cash-strapped bureaucratic structures must look for something to survive. In the backrooms of these bureaucratic structures, the prospect of war begins to look quite enticing.

David and Goliath

The blatant collusion between the Dark Forces and the governments confirms that overwhelming negative forces rule the world today. It is again the David and Goliath scenario in play, as scattered lightbearers, with little or no material force, are pitted against powerful militaristic forces backed by a monopoly of money. Yet that pebble that brought down Goliath remains in the hands of the Spiritual Hierarchy and its light forces, as we shall see below.

World Karma Leads to a Likely Scenario of War

As the suffering world remains apathetic and asleep, the Dark Forces are preparing another war that will essentially suppress all freedoms and subject the world's population to a new and even more draconian regime through their global control of gold, the only remaining money on the earth.

The aberrant $750 trillion derivative paper market that looms over the earth today will collapse, taking most of the financial and banking industry with it. It is just a matter of time before the augurs of acceleration pierce this balloon of paper value. *The cleansing of this massive debt burden is an absolute pre-condition before mankind can approach the New Age.*

Yet this collapse will lead to even more turmoil and suffering: 1) the world will sink deeper into an unprecedented economic and financial depression and 2) the Dark Force-Government collusion will conjure up a world war. Such a conflagration will most likely break out in the Middle East by year 2012.

The Dark Force Goals for the War

Plans for this major war have been on the drawing boards for decades. As part of these plans, the Iraq and Afghan Wars enabled the Dark Forces to position opposing troops in the Middle East and Central Asia. As instability grows within and without this region, the world should take note that the world's nuclear powers are now converging in this region —Iran, Russia, Pakistan, the United States, the United Kingdom, China and Israel. The Dark Forces control both warring sides, and they can easily ignite existing tensions in the Middle East into a major conflagration with wide and uncontrollable consequences.

What is planned is some sort of shock that will cause such a general outrage that the public can be led like so many sheep back into another world war. This time, however, there will be no "good guys vs. the bad ones" or the Allies vs. the Axis powers as in World War II. Instead the two opposing parties will be exposed to be two sides of the same coin.

If humanity is convinced that war in the midst of an economic depression will bring relief to its economic and financial woes, it will be walking into a trap set for its enslavement. Again, in yet another case of acquiescence, more negative karma will be added to an already overflowing world karma pot, and humanity will have to pay dearly through suffering.

On the Dark Force side, war is always an excuse to suspend basic human rights and to take more and more draconian measures to enslave the world's populace. We look to the rise of Nazi Germany and the post-World War II Stalinist pogroms in the USSR, the communist takeover of Eastern Europe, China, North Korea and North Vietnam as examples of what resulted from World War II. The war did not bring an allied victory as the history books tout but enslaved more than half of the world's population under totalitarian regimes.

An impoverished populace resulting from the worst economic depression in human history is ready fodder for the warmongers. Will men and women voluntarily line up to join the war machinery in order to feed their families? Will others be herded into government camps where the government will control what they eat, how they are clothed and when they shall sleep--all aspects of their lives?

Release of Negative Karma

This time, however, the Dark Force strategy to incite another war-for-profit will backfire. We believe that this war will ignite something akin to a karmic release that could cause the war to spread uncontrollably. Feminine energies riding on the wings of acceleration will force a rebalancing of the built-up negative karma, and this will appear to increase the intensity of the war. This rebalancing will result in great suffering to a world that has acquiesced to the Dark Forces for so long, but at the same time weaken the Dark Forces considerably.

The Dark Forces are quite familiar with the Law of Karma and from their twisted viewpoint, they will try to turn this karmic rebalancing into yet another dark opportunity to make more money as well as subject the world's population to more totalitarian control. If they must go through this karmic episode, why not profit from it and turn the whole conflict to their advantage?

At this critical point, the Dark Forces could prevail if humanity acquiesces to them. And this is the big "IF", for by the time such an outbreak takes place, the world's population will be groaning under the effects of the economic depression. Governments and the corporate world will silently agree that a war at this point will invigorate the economy while ramping up patriotic propaganda. The public could be easily manipulated into a position of silently welcoming war as a "solution" to their woes. A job in an arms factory or joining the military, for instance, will put food on the table and clothe the kids. Such a dilemma is placed before all mankind: Will it stand for light or will it acquiesce yet again to the forces of darkness?

The Spiritual Hierarchy has already determined that this war will be the last war for profit and the end to Dark Force warmongering. The Dark Forces wrongly believe that they will be able to control this episode as they have done with the countless other profitable regional conflicts.

They are, after all, masters of warfare. But this time, they will lose control to the point that the war's outcome will be left open for the light forces to determine.

As repugnant as war is, the forces of light must not err by wishing for the *status quo*. From an esoteric view the war must be seen as a karmic rebalancing that will destroy the Dark Force infrastructure of warmongering and monopolistic money control. Instead light forces must seize this opportunity to foster the total demise of the Dark Forces in the war they have created. This can be accomplished through active mental resistance on all levels of society. (See Chapter 5)

But given the apathy in the world today and the wholesale collusion between democratically elected governments and the Dark Forces, the question remains: will the forces of light and the general public be able to muster the wherewithal to direct the outcome of such a war?

Humanity's Option

Mankind can determine the *outcome* of such a war: it can resist all Dark Forces attempts to drag it into war. This resistance must come from all levels of the society and can be both mental and physical. However, given the present overwhelming earthly odds against scattered light forces, mankind must appeal to the Spiritual Hierarchy for help. But what does mankind know of the Spiritual Hierarchy today? The answer is: virtually nothing. Today, the world in general is almost totally ignorant of the existence of the Spiritual Hierarchy, the only force that can save them from this situation. This is why the lightbearers are so important because they are supposed to be the earthly representatives of the Spiritual Hierarchy at this critical juncture and must bring this information to their communities.

Even if the world is forced into a world war, the more public opinion mentally opposes war and invokes the helping hand of the Spiritual Hierarchy, the shorter the conflagration will be. But if a major part of humanity acquiesces to the war and builds more negative karma by looking upon it, either consciously or subconsciously, as a panacea for their economic and financial problems, then the war will drag on, and the world will suffer greatly. A world population opposing each other as to the legitimacy of the war is the ideal situation for the Dark Forces. "Divide and conquer" is their motto.

The Spiritual Hierarchy's Option

So we stand at a similar point on the sidereal cycle, when, at the end of a previous Earth Year, Atlantis was given the choice to sink or reform their ways. At that point, they had developed a technology using sound as a weapon; and when aimed at human beings, it could cause the body's organs to explode. It was a technology, not unlike our lasers today. Moreover, they discovered that by accumulating money for power and warmongering, they could control the masses. Due to their recalcitrance, the governing bodies of the Brotherhood of Light saw no alternative but to sink the continent and start anew.

These same reincarnated Atlanteans have exerted the same regime on the world today, and we again face the same choice: give up the monopoly of money and renounce warmongering or sink. Instead we see only defiance. So, we stand precariously at the same cliff's edge as Atlantis before its destruction. They made their choice, and the rest is cosmic history.

Between a Rock and a Hard Place

If the coming world war plays out in favour of the Dark Forces and mankind remains sheep-like, apathetic, fearful and acquiescent, humanity's entry into the New Age will be at stake. To stop them, the light forces will need to invoke divine help which may consist of "catastrophic" earth changes in order to deal a final blow to the major part of Dark Force infrastructure and cities. This is why the forces of light may find themselves between "a rock and a hard place", that is, invoking devastating earth changes to deal the final blow to the Dark Forces, knowing at the same time the human suffering of such a blow. The world must face this tough decision and must come to realize that there are greater issues than one's personal, selfish safety and needs. What is at stake is mankind's evolution and entry into a much better era of great promise.

In response to the threat of catastrophic earth changes, the Dark Forces have made it known that they, too, have the power to inflict earth changes in the form of earthquakes and directed weather patterns such as

41

hurricanes, cyclones, and floods.   Do they really?   Their arrogance is without limit.

The Trump Card

The Spiritual Hierarchy has always held the cosmic trump card with respect to errant civilisations.   It has had to use this trump card to sink the Lemurian and Atlantean civilizations in order to prevent them from reaching their peaks of evil.   So earth changes are not only invoked to cleanse the physical earth of pollution and environmental decay but also to rectify deeply entrenched moral wrongs conjured up by the various Root-Races, a situation in which we find ourselves today.

We believe that the trump card today consists of a worldwide deluge.   This time, enormous land-based ice sheets, perched on the continent of Antarctica and on Greenland in the Arctic, risk sliding into the sea causing a significant rise to global sea levels.   The general warming of the earth has caused these massive ice sheets to break away from the main land glaciers and to slide toward the ocean. Recently, scientists have observed that as the ice sheets slide, friction between the ground and the moving ice sheets generates heat and creates a complex "plumbing system" of meltwater rivers, lakes and streams under the ice sheets.   This meltwater "greases" the movement of the ice sheets toward the ocean at an even greater speed.

The scientific and political world should not content itself with the idea that it will take centuries for the two polar ice caps to melt in order to cause any significant rise in the sea levels.   The ice sheets can slide into the sea and raise sea level catastrophically through displacement within a matter of days.[1]

Also models of the potential rise in the earth's sea level have ignored the effects of the sub-glacial meltwater phenomenon and the vast streams of ice pouring into sea under the ice sheets. Already, islands off the coast of India have been submerged. The Republic of Kiribati other island countries in the South Pacific, the Maldives in Indian Ocean are already disappearing under rising sea levels. Their populations are quietly being evacuated to neighbouring continental countries.

If these ice sheets slip into the ocean, it is estimated that the *global* sea level will rise more than 200 feet or about 65 meters in a matter of days. Scientific American[2] estimates that three principal ice sheets can potentially slip into the sea and cause the following increase in sea levels:

West Antarctic = 19 ft / 6 m sea level rise.

Greenland = 24 ft / 7.3 m sea level rise.

East Antarctic = 170 ft / 52 m sea level rise

With the mere command of the Mahachohan in the Spiritual Hierarchy, powerful energies can be focused on

---

[1] Robin E. Bell, Director Center for Rivers and Estuaries, Columbia University Earth Institute, "Unquiet Ice Unquiet Ice Speaks Volumes on Global Warming"," *Scientific American*, no. 298.2 (2008) pp. 60-67.

[2] Ibid.

these ice sheets to make them slip into the sea. Again, we do not have to wait centuries for the ice to melt for sea levels to rise. The displacement of these huge masses of land-based ice can cause a significant rise in the sea level in a matter of days, covering all major coastal cities and inundating all the financial capitals of the world, including New York, London, Dubai, Singapore, Mumbai, Hong Kong, Toronto and Shanghai. The Spiritual Hierarchy can release this action if it becomes clear that mankind cannot or does not want to muster the light necessary to defeat the Dark Forces.

Government propaganda promoting complacency about rising sea levels must be discounted, and the eventual slippage of these ice sheets into the sea is already at a critical stage.

A Word to the Wise

The battle between the light and dark forces was never meant to be easy, and as we have observed since the global financial crisis began, the Dark Forces will not go down without a battle royal. But the true governing bodies of earth, the Spiritual Hierarchy, will not permit the Dark Forces to enter the New Age with the rest of humanity, so until they are completely annihilated, we must wait at the threshold of the New Age.

By the time the war starts, all paper monetary instruments and currencies will have lost significant value, and a period of confusion about money will follow. With their huge stores of gold, the Dark Forces will hold a monopoly on power, and with this power they will begin the implementation of their plans to enslave mankind.

In Volume 1 we strongly recommended that the reader begin accumulating minted gold and silver coins. Then in 2001, these gold and silver coins were valued at USD 270 and USD 6.00 per one ounce piece respectively. Today they are worth about USD1200 and USD25.00 per one ounce piece respectively. Still, this increase, although significant, should not deter today's readers from taking all measures possible to accumulate these coins as best they can. Compared to what will come about in the future, these coins are still cheap.

Those holding silver and gold will be able to maintain their independence against the growing encroachment on their basic rights and liberties. They can also serve humanity by helping those less fortunate. Those without these precious metals must resort to barter or government handouts and will become subject to their control.

Many starry-eyed New Agers discount the value of silver and gold, not wanting to have anything to do with this "filthy lucre". They think that they are under the protection of God and that somehow all their needs will be met no matter what. It is true that the divine meets all needs, only if one takes the first step. The Master St. Germain's advice more than ten years ago was to begin acquiring these precious metals for use in this period of turmoil.

Acquire these metals coin by coin if need be, and this very effort will invite divine help. But if you do nothing despite these admonitions, then you will just suffer the consequences. What more can the Spiritual Hierarchy do than to give you valid information upon which to act?

Once the richest nation in the world, the United States has been milked dry. It exists on the quicksand of debt. Other nations follow right behind. To the Dark Forces, the nation-state has always been just a convenient unit of wealth extraction, and the financial system, primarily through the derivative market, is designed to drain the coffers of both the individual and the nation-states who have any resources left. But to what end, you might ask? Toward two very unenlightened and narrow goals: monopoly of power and the subjugation of humanity.

The concentration of power and money is tending toward China, the most solvent country in the world. China has accumulated vast stores silver because it has served as the primary means of exchange for centuries. It would take a simple declaration that China will back its currency with silver to bring the entire world of fiat currencies to its knees. This is how fragile and volatile the current financial system is today. This possibility hovers over the earth today as yet another sub-strategy of the Dark Forces' exit policy.

Spot Insurrections and Revolts Ahead

In the years to come, as the public is subjected to more and more suffering at the hands of their governments and the ever deepening economic depression, more public unrest is in store. Very much aware of this possibility, the forces of darkness have installed measures to put down protests and revolts, i.e. to quell any resistance to their draconian measures.

Public security measures and equipment have already been put into place in anticipation of the certain unrest that a deep economic depression will bring. People have already been reduced to sheep as they pass through airport, train and building security check points where they are forcibly searched under penalty of imprisonment. It remains to be seen to what degree an impoverished population will be able to resist further measures.

So besides the prospect of World War III, internal upheaval within countries is also brewing. Will this be sufficient to overturn the hegemony the Dark Forces exercise over the world's populations?

Vigilance and Perspicacity Required

The Dark Forces are of all races and imbedded in positions of power and money in all countries of the world. They are American, European, South American, Arab, Indian, African, Chinese, Pakistani, Iranian, etc. as we have witnessed in the global banking and governmental systems. These forces move about the earth as if there were no borders. The nation-state is their unit of victimization, and their infiltration into all governments is a fact and baldly paraded before the public.

The Dark Forces are highly intelligent albeit of a low spiritual nature, and through their black magicians and their growing monopoly of gold, they will attempt to drag mankind down as they exit. It is sort of a global hostage-taking strategy.

We must be cautious and discreet in our movements and activities and realize that they still wield enormous physical power that might even result in extra-terrestrial intervention if needed.

The control of information via the mass media is firmly in the hands of the Dark Forces, so all news items must be regarded as mental manipulation designed to herd the public in a desired direction. To counter this control, the Internet, an innovation that the Master St. Germain so wisely introduced to the world, has played a large role in decentralizing information, and more and more of the public is being awakened.

Vigilance is necessary because the damage the Dark Forces can inflict on the earth and humanity during their forced exit may be incalculable. But if humanity rises up *mentally* against these demonic efforts, the Spiritual Hierarchy will back it with sure fire and the promise that Light will prevail in this last battle between light and darkness will be fulfilled. (See Chapter 5 Mobilization of the Light Forces)

Conclusion

As the current global crisis has played out so far, it is clear that humanity has chosen the more difficult path. The mental bodies of both the earth and its inhabitants remain weak and ill, and the rebalancing of the world will take longer than anticipated. Even after the Dark Forces have been severely weakened and eliminated from their thrones of militaristic power and money, the minds of mankind must undergo a radical shift from the thinking of the current civilisation to one that is more in line with the Divine Plan. The Spiritual Hierarchy estimates that around 2050 to 2060, the rebalancing of the earth will hopefully be achieved, and the earth will be ready to enter the New Age.

So those who long for a return to "normality" will never see it again. What has passed is the past. What has gone bankrupt is bankrupt. What has crumbled is crumbled. Those who move in tandem with the great changes of this waning cycle will survive and later like the phoenix rising out of the ashes of destruction, will build the New Age.

Evolution marches on. Even while turmoil grips the world, pockets of hope in the Spiritual Regions will begin to form and the seeds of the New Age will be planted.

Chapter 2

Havens of Hope in Turmoil

High above the struggle on the earth's populated coastal and lowland regions, the seeds of a new civilization are already beginning to sprout in some of the twelve Spiritual Regions around the globe. The Spiritual Hierarchy has provided mankind an opportunity to continue its evolutionary journey unabated in these regions, away from the turmoil of worldwide flooding. In the safety of these Spiritual Regions, acceleration will continue to urge on the evolution of mankind. The Spiritual Hierarchy, earth's true inner government of the earth, has always provided a fast track of evolution known as the Path of Initiation. Souls are given the opportunity to evolve spiritually at a faster pace than humanity in general. Through a process of natural migration, advanced souls, lightbearers and incarnations of the incoming Sixth Root-Race will congregate in the Spiritual Regions to experiment with a transitional society that will preserve the good of the present waning society and synthesize it with individual and group soul expression. The prototype that emerges will serve as a model society for entering the New Age. Thus the light of the soul will gradually emerge as the predominant force of development in the Spiritual Regions spurred on by the continued acceleration of energies.

As the light of the soul emerges through each lightbearer's physical body, these lightbearers will guide the reconstruction of a society based on cosmic laws the soul innately understands. Just as the soul governs the individual, so will cosmic law govern the new transitional society.

The general population outside the Spiritual Regions will experience the upheavals caused by rising sea levels and economic unrest. Inhabitants of the Spiritual Regions should selflessly serve the flood-affected populations and hopefully put them back upon the surer path of spiritual evolution.

In line with the Divine Plan, the Spiritual Regions will be the first to evolve from a third to fourth dimensional existence over the coming centuries. This is the direction of mankind's evolution, but first, it must hurdle the next fifty or so years of earthly readjustment following the exit of the Dark Forces.

The Divine Plan for the Fourth Round

We mentioned in Volume 2 that we had come to the end of the fourth *sub-round* and are entering the fifth sub-round within the Fourth Round. This coincides with crossing the mid-point of the Fourth Round and concludes humanity's episode in the most concrete form of physical existence. Human evolution now points upward toward the completion of the second half of the Fourth Round. During this evolutionary, our existence will gradually move from the dense physical to the etheric plane, and by the end of the Fourth Round, we will have passed through the fifth, sixth and seventh *sub-rounds*, and cast off our concrete bodies in favour of more etheric bodies of the advanced Seventh Root-Race.

The Sixth Root-Race is already incarnating all around the world, overlapping the present waning Fifth Root-Race which has already been in existence for over one million years. When the Sixth Root-Race also reaches its zenith and begins to wane, perhaps in another million years, the Seventh Root-Race will appear and carry us to the end of the Fourth Round. The whole concrete physical plane that we know today will have been cast off and mankind will exist in bodies made up of refined etheric material in an equally etheric environment.

After humanity reaches this totally etheric existence, we will enter a major pralaya, and the earth will either be destroyed or will go into limbo like our moon. Our souls will go into a long rest period after which they will reincarnate in higher etheric forms, most probably made of mental substance, to start the Fifth Round on another planetary body within one of many solar systems in the Universe. *Grosso modo*, this is the Divine Plan for the second half of the Fourth Round.

The Next Step—The Fifth Sub-Round of the Fourth Round

As we mentioned above, the continued acceleration of energies will speed up humanity's upward climb into the fifth sub-round of the Fourth Round. How long mankind will stay in the fifth sub-round will depend on its spiritual progress. But as acceleration will continue unabated, it is unlikely that our stay in the next sub-round will drag on as long as it has in the fourth sub-round.

We are entering the minor pralaya that lies between the fourth and fifth sub-rounds. This minor pralaya also corresponds to what some esoterists call the "Thousand Years of Peace" or the Golden Age. In reality, it is the winding down of the present civilisation where a re-evaluation takes place and its good and positive aspects, i.e. all that serve mankind, are retained. Two more generations of Sixth Root-Race will incarnate will be more open and transparent to the higher dimensions and the teachings of the Spiritual Hierarchy.

So the "everyone-for-himself" syndrome that so characterizes our civilisation today will hopefully be transformed into a more giving and sharing society where the "God Within" begins to emerge as the prime motivating element of human action instead of ambition, power, money and fame. Once this rebalancing covers the earth, we will then be ready to face the evolutionary challenges and lessons that await us in the fifth-sub-round of the Fourth Round.

The Geographical Locations of the Spiritual Regions

In volume 2 of *The Sanctus Germanus Prophecies*, we indicated that during the post-2012 period of climate and earth changes, twelve geographical regions would evolve into Spiritual Regions where lightbearers, in close contact with adepts and Masters of the Spiritual Hierarchy, would carry out the Divine Plan. To recapitulate, these Spiritual Regions are as follows:

North America: (1) Banff-Lake Louise area in the Canadian Rockies to the Grand Tetons of Wyoming, USA and (2) the Colorado Plateau in the USA.

South America: (3) The Cordoba Province Uritorco/Capilla del Monte region in Argentina and (4) Goias Province in Brazil

Asia: (5) Qinghai-Tibet Plateau and (6) Gobi Desert Plateau

South Asia: (7) the Darjeeling District (including Sikkim) in the Himalayas

Australia: (8) the Australian Outback region

Middle East: (9) Iran plateau near Yazd, Iran

Africa: (10) Central Highlands of the Lake Kivu area and (11) the Ahaggar Plateau near Tamanrasset, Algeria

Europe: (12) Transylvanian Plateau in the Carpathian Mountains

Again, Spiritual Regions should not be confused with the high altitude safe zones which will also be spared flooding caused by the rising sea levels. Flooding in the coastal and lowland areas will force displacement of their populations to these neighbouring higher altitude safe zones.

Each Spiritual Region is endowed with higher vibrational energies that will enable more direct communication with the Spiritual Hierarchy in Shambhalla. In each Spiritual Region there are high vibrational energy portals that will, in time, be revealed to their residents. A few advanced initiates in each Spiritual Regions already know where these portals are located and await the time when their disciples can be trusted with this information. In time these portals will be endowed with a shrine or temple where people can meditate or be healed.

Not all Spiritual Regions are the Same

Each Spiritual Region is currently undergoing a purification process as the Spiritual Hierarchy focuses high-energy feminine vibrations into these regions. As a result, this will cause great upheavals in some while others will begin to organize for their future roles in the Divine Plan.

Some Spiritual Regions are already drawing in populations of lightbearers, while still others are due for major cleansing. It is said that in some Spiritual Regions, groups of adepts and initiates already live and work on the etheric plane. For example, the Iranian Plateau is inaccessible due to political and ingrained religious reasons but this does not stop secret societies from preparing for the future. The Darjeeling District in the Himalayas is currently undergoing a cleansing while the Lake Kivu area including Goma, Congo must recover from the most heinous of human crimes, genocide, and the aftermath of military rampages and pillaging. The urban areas of the Colorado Plateau are still too overpopulated and polluted while the Banff and Lake Louise area of the Canadian Rockies have been mercifully preserved their pristine state because they are located in a protected national park. Thus those Spiritual Regions that are relatively pristine in nature and the least affected by rank materialism or war will advance first.

Populating the Spiritual Regions

During the decade of turmoil from 2007 to 2017, lightbearers who respond to their soul callings will gravitate to the twelve Spiritual Regions. This natural migration is implanted in their souls as part of the Divine Plan. Incoming lightbearers will meet other like-minded lightbearers who bring their expertise and visions of a future society. Together they will begin the reconstruction effort by creating a transitional society that will function as the bridge between the Spiritual Hierarchy and the populations in the surrounding regions.

Unconscious and Conscious Migration

As the turmoil and tumult of both human conflict and earth changes accelerate, lightbearers from all corners of the world will be naturally drawn to the Spiritual Regions. This migration is presently taking place, some consciously some unconsciously, and will increase as individual soul urgings become more apparent and urgent. When the Dark Forces unleash the next World War, this will trigger earth changes, and the combination of the two will awaken many souls to migrate elsewhere.

Each person must find and define his or her place in the Spiritual Region's divine plan as it is written in the individual soul plan. Finding, defining and implementing this individual soul plan and determining how it fits into the Spiritual Region's plan are of primary importance and the subject of Chapter 6.

Once implanted in a Spiritual Region, lightbearers are expected to know their mission and their place in the Divine Plan of the Spiritual Region. There will be no welcoming committee to greet and help them settle in, and although the right resources will be put into place according to the Divine Plan, lightbearers will be expected to initiate action of their own particular soul mission before the Brotherhood will release any further resources. They will take on projects to teach and inform people of the coming events and how to prepare for them.

The move into a Spiritual Region is not meant to be a comfortable safe spot for retirement or a cushy material life. Too many times, lightbearers want a guaranteed job and salary before they will move to a new environment, for it seems that the pioneer spirit has been squelched by too "cushy" a material life in the present location. Many lightbearers risk not responding to their soul urgings and give in to the fear of uprooting themselves from their comfortable surroundings to one that is unknown. At the same time, the Spiritual Hierarchy will not issue any guarantees unless lightbearers take the first step, with the utmost faith, conviction and commitment to pursue their Path.

Along the path, the Spiritual Hierarchy will meet them at numerous junctures to quench their thirst and replenish them. But even so, lightbearers should not expect the Masters to coddle them if they decide to move into one of the Spiritual Regions. Lightbearers are merely expected to do what they promised to do prior to this incarnation.

Cosmic Laws of Attraction and Hierarchy

The differences between the Spiritual Regions and the areas around them are vibrational. Individuals whose vibrations are compatible with the Spiritual Regions' will be drawn there in accordance with the Law of Attraction which attracts like vibrations but does not exclude. There will be no walls or fences to separate the Regions from the rest of the world.

The Law of Attraction will also determine with whom lightbearers will group within a particular Spiritual Region. Every individual brings ingrained personal and psychological tendencies that may not jibe with group action. This will be an ongoing challenge but a natural coming together of like-minded people should take place and on the basis of this compatibility groups should be formed.

The cosmic Law of Hierarchy will govern the structure of the group in the Spiritual Regions and how it functions. The Master Serapis Bey speaks of the Law of Hierarchy as:

"(It is) that structure which exists in all form, in all nature, and in all creation . . . It is the ascending and descending of angels. It is that great and holy feeling one gets when one gazes upon one's teacher, and it is a deep compassion that comes from being deep with one's own student. Hierarchy indeed! Little understood in the West, a way of life in the East. In any given area there will always be your Hierarch, the one who looms above you, from whose sight you may attain grace and benefits. It is but the immature who resent this thing--those who have not yet outgrown the arrogance that comes from ignorance, and would always be the leader of the pack.

And yet I say Hierarchy is misunderstood, very misunderstood in the West, for here you find yourself paying obeisance to those who do not lead but actually should be following you. And to those who do lead and in truth are your Hierarchs, you pay no mind at times, ignoring them, at times criticizing them as well. Ah! Let there be a mighty healing in this land, and let it come from the West unto the East.

. . . (I) t is of vital importance that you grasp this, for in grasping it you have the key to harmonious human relationships. You who have spoken of problems with others, you who have offended or been offended, these have all come from blindness of hierarchical structure and nothing else. For if you understand and grasp this plainly, you will see to whom you are accountable and who is accountable to you. To the former, you will be respectful, and to the latter, gracious. So be it! So be it always! For I tell you that until you grasp this lesson cleanly, you may not enter the planes of heaven, and this is not exclusion by the Divine Hand, but simply a matter of vibrational realities that persist and endure always in the invisible worlds. One automatically resonates and thus inhabits that realm to which one most appropriately belongs; neither higher, neither lower.[3]

People working under similar vibrations can accomplish much more with the best, efficient use of energy. Opposing and resisting one's group actions or leader drains the group of vitality and purpose. Those who wish to kibitz and criticize their group's actions should move on and join other groups more compatible with their ideas and vibrations.

---

[3] Serapis Bey's communication to the students of the Sanctus Germanus Foundation.

Guiding Principle: Soul Contact

Lightbearers represent the core of the future organization in the Spiritual Regions and to a greater extent, the world.   They must re-learn to turn inward and integrate their souls with their personalities so that the soul plans inscribed within will manifest through their physical vehicles. This is the essence of Soul Liberation. This guiding principle was laid down centuries ago in the sacred yoga sutras of Patanjali and will continue to serve with the same validity and authority in the Spiritual Regions under the overall guidance of the Master St. Germain.

So widespread will be the turmoil on earth that no human organization (e.g. the Red Cross, NGO's, national governments etc) can possibly help or guide people adequately. To lightbearers who establish soul contact, an organized plan with the necessary resources will manifest from the soul.   Once the lightbearer takes the first steps to implement his or her plan, then the adepts and initiates of the Spiritual Hierarchy will make contact and offer their help and guidance.   These latter will not appear in turbans or archaic clothes but as ordinary humans.   At first lightbearers will not realize who they are, but over time and observations, they will come to know with whom they are working.   In chaos, then, *lightbearer soul contact will be the only organized way that the earth populations will realize the leadership they need to re-establish their footing.*

Each individual soul plan makes up a part of the whole Divine Plan, and the extent to which the lightbearer achieves soul contact will determine how these individual plans honeycomb together to bring about a new society.

Basic Functions of the Spiritual Regions

In volumes 1 and 2 of *The Sanctus Germanus Prophecies* we covered some of the functions of the transitional society that will develop in the Spiritual Regions. In this section we will provide additional information that has been revealed to us since those two volumes were published.

Development in the Spiritual Regions, if in line with the Divine Plan, will evolve from a third to a fourth dimensional existence over the coming centuries. This is the compelling long-term direction of mankind's evolution, but first, mankind must hurdle the next five to six decades of turmoil and earthly readjustment following the exit of the Dark Forces.

Much of the development of the Spiritual Regions will be left to the inhabitants to determine in line with the Cosmic Law of Free Will. They will determine which policies, traditional habitudes, ideas or technologies will serve or do not serve. Bringing forth their experiences from our present civilization, lightbearers, who have been incarnating over the past fifty years, will bridge the present and future civilizations.

The Spiritual Hierarchy's Role

In line with the prophecy that the Master Djwal Khul advanced through Alice A. Bailey, the externalization of the Hierarchy, which has already begun, will intensify in the Spiritual Regions.

Great centers of occult learning and research will develop under the Spiritual Hierarchy's vortices in each Spiritual Region. New teachings, pertinent to entering the New Age, will emanate from Shambhalla, the Spiritual Hierarchy's etheric nerve centre, and flow into the Spiritual Regions. The Masters will teach and disseminate the hierarchy's teachings directly or through high level initiates.

Spiritual Region teaching centers, like those of ancient times, will maintain great ancient and modern occult works in archives that will assure the continuity of the Ancient Wisdom. Education to overcome ignorance of cosmic laws has always been the backbone of the Spiritual Hierarchy's externalization effort, for as the Master Saint Germain has said on countless occasions, "If they knew better, they would do better."

As the New Age involves changing our dimension of existence, from the third to the fourth dimension, changing and learning to live in a higher dimension—the fourth—will require a different set of teachings that the Spiritual Hierarchy will gradually hand down to humanity through the avatars and initiates who have volunteered for this ominous task. We say ominous because many such teachers have met with violent and fatal resistance from mankind and a quick appointment with the tombstone.

The teachings leading to a fourth dimensional existence will be entrusted to advanced initiates in the

Spiritual Regions who will determine when such information can be released to the greater public.

Preservation of Exoteric and Esoteric Archives

Archival holdings handed down over the ages will form the basis of the Brotherhood's teachings, for no longer will false prophets be able to invent teachings at will without their audience having at their disposal volumes of the Ageless Wisdom to either verify or invalidate that which is being said or taught. The need for this underpinning has never been greater in this world of great media expansion, fuelled by false prophecy and dodgy mediums.

Regional mystic archives and libraries, protected from the vagaries of climate and human fickleness, will form the foundation of all human endeavour. Cosmic Law, the basis of all spiritual and religious thought, will prevail.

Spread of the Brotherhood's Teachings

Lightbearers and new disciples on the Path will go forth from these centers in the Spiritual Regions to teach those among the surviving populations who want to listen. Making use of modern communications techniques that will survive the earthly upheavals, Spiritual Regions will disseminate the Brotherhood's teachings to the masses of humanity which will be, like no other time, more receptive to such teachings.

Liberating the Spiritual Regions and Creating New Models of Civilization

The world from which we are emerging is a regime in which the Dark Forces control energy through a monopoly of the petroleum, gas, coal, electricity sectors, money (paper and electronic) through the world's central banks and banking industry, health through the drug and health care industry, information through the mass media, food through the giant food transport and distribution systems, clothing through mass sweat shops and distribution networks, transportation of all types and housing through the banking and mortgage system. In addition, they maintain leverage on governmental bodies by supporting them through loans and other forms of payments and controlling the tax revenue bodies. This is the tight grip instituted in today's society that stymies soul expression through the outer physical body in the physical world. By using the New Age movement commercialize spiritual teachings, the Dark Forces have tried to twist the teachings of the Ancient Wisdom to suit this grip. An example of this would be the commercialization of the Law of Attraction to satisfy the ego's desire to get rich.

The control of the above sectors constitutes the modern-day shackles to human and soul liberation. In the Divine Plan for mankind, NONE of these shackles exists. Thus the first major challenge facing the populations in the Spiritual Regions is to break the control of all the above areas. The global financial crisis, war, and earth changes will play a role in liberating the Spiritual Regions from the grip of the Dark Forces. Chaos is a great liberator, for as national governments become more and more embroiled in saving themselves, prosecuting war, and dealing with critical earth crises, the people will find opportunities to take back control over their own local economies, including power generation, local food production, health services, and other necessities.

Community development models growing out of the experiments and which have achieved sustainability will spread to the neighbouring areas creating a snowball effect of ideas. By roughly 2050 to 2060, most communities will have liberated themselves, and the peoples of the earth will have come to realize how the Dark Forces had hijacked key segments of their lives for their own enrichment.

Free Energy

The powerful countrywide and international electric grid systems that the Dark Forces currently control will be challenged more and more by the incoming floods and geological changes. The Spiritual Regions should negotiate the return of local hydroelectric and power generating plants, including alternative power sources of power, from global conglomerates. In other words, they should decouple local power generating plants from the wider grid.

Local power generation is a temporary measure that will allow time for the development of free energy. Free energy is derived from tapping into the earth's magnetic grid to create alternating magnetic attractions that run machines, much like alternating electrical energy is used to turn electric motors.

A new paradigm based on free energy is currently fomenting. Private inventors have already produced machines that can turn in perpetuity, and it will be a matter of time before these free energy machines will be turning electric generators locally. The civilization need not march backward just because the towers of finance, warmongering and energy crumble. There are other sources of energy that can keep the electric grid full of electricity. The Spiritual Regions will be at the vanguard of those areas on earth which achieve complete use of free energy.

Local Coinage of Silver and Gold

As the national and international banking systems crumble, the Spiritual Regions will re-establish gold and silver as a medium of exchange for goods and services. Below is an explanation of the function of gold, not only as a means of exchange, but carrying broader benefits for the society in general:

Gold was a common commodity. . in all Golden Ages, because its natural emanation is a purifying, balancing, and vitalizing energy or force. It is placed within the earth by the "Lords to Creation "-- those "Great Beings of Life and Love" who create and direct worlds, systems of worlds, and the expansion of the light in the beings upon them.

The outer or intellectual knowledge of humanity holds within it little--very little--understanding of the real purpose for which gold exists on this planet. It grows within the earth like a plant, and through it there is constantly pouring a purifying, vitalizing, and balancing current of energy into the very ground we walk upon, as well as into the growth of nature and the atmosphere we breathe.

Gold is placed upon this planet for a variety of uses, two of its most trivial and unimportant ones being that of using gold as a means of exchange and for ornamentation. The far greater activity and purpose of it, within and upon the earth, is the release of its own inherent quality and energy to purify, vitalize and balance the atomic structure of the world.

The scientific world today has no inkling as yet of this activity. However, it serves the same purpose to our earth that radiators do to our homes. Gold is one of the most important ways by which the energy from our sun is supplied to the interior of the earth, and the balance of activities maintained. As a conveyor of this energy, it acts as a transformer to pass the sun's force into the physical substance of our world, as well as to the life evolving upon it. The energy within gold is really the radiant, electronic force from the sun, acting in a lower octave. Gold is sometimes called a precipitated sun-ray.

As the energy within gold is of extremely high vibratory rate, it can only act upon the finer and more subtle expressions of life, through absorption. In all

"Golden Ages," this metal comes into plentiful and common use by the mass of the people, and whenever such a condition occurs, the spiritual development of that people reaches of very high state. In these ages, the gold is never hoarded but instead, is widely distributed into the use of the masses who, absorbing its purifying energy, are themselves raised into greater perfection. Such is the right use of gold, and when this Law is consciously understood and obeyed, the individual may draw any quantity he desires to himself by the use of that Law.

Because of the gold deposits in all mountain ranges, one finds health and vigour in life upon the mountains that he cannot find in any other places on the earth's surface. No one ever heard of detrimental effects coming to those who constantly handle pure gold. While in its pure state, it is soft and wears away easily; still the very quality is the fulfilling of this purpose of which I have just spoken.

The more advanced of these people produced much gold by precipitation direct from the Universal. The domes of many buildings were covered with sheets of pure gold and the interiors decorated with brilliant jewels in curious yet marvellous designs. These jewels were also precipitated--direct from the One Eternal Substance.[4]

---

[4] From King, Godfre Ray, Unveiled Mysteries , Saint Germain Foundation Inc., pp. 44-46

Humanity has not yet learned how to handle money and has allowed the wholesale hijacking of this vital function into the hands of the Dark Forces. Little do they know that the more gold they hoard, the more it will purify and rebalance the preponderant masculine energies they use to control the world. The more gold circulates within the Spiritual Regions, the more it will add to the vitality, purification and rebalancing of the region.

As for gold's trivial function as a means of exchange, the global financial crisis marks the end of an era of the misuse of money and its control by the banking system. Learning to handle gold as money is an objective for the next five decades, a unique feature of life on planet earth. So the Spiritual Regions must return to "grade one" of the school of money until its population learns its use and function.

The power of the means of exchange (money and barter) will return to the people through the free coinage of silver and gold. Those who are able to coin their silver and gold metals through a mint in a Spiritual Region will gradually introduce coins into a local barter system, exchanging them for goods and services. Thus the initial circulation of gold or silver will spread as a means to equalize barter differences.

People will also be able to find gold in nature. The spiritually advanced will be able to precipitate it for others to use. In either case, they will then bring it to a mint which will strike standard coins that will be recognized anywhere in the world not because of the design or head of authority struck on them but for the purity of metal content. Thus will begin another human episode where gold will return into circulation as the basis for exchange.

The extent to which gold circulates and is freely used among the people in a Spiritual Region will serve as a barometer of the level of spiritual progress achieved among its population.

Taxation

The Dark Forces have committed the most egregious crimes against humanity through the well-developed taxation systems developed under the nation-state system. We mentioned in volume 1 that the tax revenue services of most of the world's countries have never been audited or made accountable for what they collect. Through this system they have been able "to skim their share off the top" before handing the governments the rest of the crumbs, thus transferring enormous wealth from the people to their warmongering operations.

The Spiritual Regions must rethink the whole concept of taxation. What it has become today is official theft and misuse to support the growth of bureaucracy.

Health

Lightbearers and new disciples on the Path will go forth from these Spiritual Regions to teach the surviving populations the great promise that the Master Jesus gave to the world. "Physician, heal thyself." Self-healing methods that already exist will be disseminated, and the health industry that has profited so much from the sick will be discarded. New, inexpensive remedies with wide spectra of effectiveness will come to light and will be self-administered, giving back to the individual full control over his or her health.

Manufactured diseases designed to enrich the pharmaceutical industry will be exposed and control of one's health will return to the individual.

Education of Sixth Root-Race Children

It is likely that the children born to lightbearers in the Spiritual Regions will incarnate in Sixth Root-Race bodies and will need radically different educational systems from what we have now. The Sixth Root-Race started incarnating all around the world in greater numbers from 1960 onward, and it is likely that these early incarnations would be best suited to serve as the educators of these children.

The present crop of lightbearers is likely to be mixture of both the seventh sub-race of the Fifth Root-Race and the first sub-race of the Sixth. They are both endowed with a natural ability to access other dimensions and are generally highly intelligent, so much so that they naturally refuse to be pigeonholed into an educational system based on the "3R's". The former tend to be older and more involved with trying to reform the current health and educational systems for the sake of their Sixth Root-Race children, while the latter are the early "volunteers" of the Sixth Root-Race and have made the difficult transition through the concrete-minded health and school systems.

Many have been severely damaged by the present system as it aggressively tried to force them into conformity with the present world through drugs. Others were lucky to incarnate into good families who protected and educated them, easing their adaptation in the Fifth Root-Race world. These latter, if drawn to the Spiritual Regions, would comprise the core of teachers that would devise a proper education environment for the incoming Sixth Root-Race children of lightbearer parents in the Spiritual Regions.

The Sixth Root-Race is the wave of the future. Their openness to the higher dimensions is both a blessing and a hardship in this period of transition. On one hand, they possess a natural leaning toward the spiritual teachings of the Spiritual Hierarchy while on the other hand, they can become easy victims of capricious astral plane entities. Being able to exist consciously on two or three planes at a time takes much discernment and understanding of the occult world, so the education program, for Sixth Root-Race would lean much on a better understanding of that inner world that occultists so cherish.

Surviving the Floods

It goes without saying that lightbearers responding to their deep soul missions will most likely be among the survivors, for they incarnated expressly to be here for this great transition and are key to the implementation of the Divine Plan. However, what about the rest of the world's population?

Monads of the Lunar *Pitris*—The Likely Survivors

Those who survive these tumultuous events will most likely be incarnations of what esoterists call the lunar *pitri* monads. Helena P. Blavatsky, in *The Secret Doctrine*, revealed that the moon, considered by modern astronomers as a satellite of the planet earth, is actually earth's parent.[5] At the end of its last planetary Round, the moon became a wasteland in the process of self-destruction. Its inhabitants returned to their monad forms and went into a grand *pralaya* or rest period only to emerge on the planet earth to continue their journey of evolution.

These monads, H.P. Blavatsky defines as follows:

> The Progenitors of Man, called in India "Fathers," Pitara or *Pitris*, are the creators of our bodies and lower principles. They are ourselves, as the first personalities, and we are they. Primeval man would be "the bone of their bone and the flesh of their flesh," if they had body and flesh. As stated, they were "lunar Beings.[6]

We can infer from this quote that since this stock of lunar *pitri* monads represents the original and ever evolving group of monads, of which we are a part, that

---

[5] For an explanation of the interplay between the Lunar Chain and the Earth Chain of globes, see HPB, *The Secret Doctrine, vol. 1* pp. 173-175.

[6] Blavatsky, HP. *The Secret Doctrine*, v. 2, 1.1 Stanza 4, Adyar: The Theosophical Society Vasanta Press, p. 88

they will survive the great shocks in the coming decades as part of their evolutionary journey on earth.

Referring to the diagram in Vol. 2 of the Grand Cycle, the monads which took form from the First Round to the Fourth Round, experienced millions of years of involution. From ethereal creatures they gradually compacted into the flesh and bone human beings we are today. In the Fourth Round which takes place on the planet earth, these monads then formed into the Fifth Root-Race, an involutionary process that made the human form smaller and more compact (i.e. densely material) over millions of years.

Around 400 years ago, these monads, by this time wearing concrete Fifth Root-Race bodies, reached the half-way point of the Grand Cycle and from that point onward, the process of evolution began reversing the process of compaction.

The human bodies we wear today represent slightly less dense ones than those of 400 years ago and are the last stage of the Fifth Root-Race. Overlapping this last stage is the incoming Sixth Root-Race. So what we will experience over the next couple of centuries is the gradual takeover of the first sub-race of the Sixth Root-Race which will carry us into the next fifth sub-round of the Fourth Round.

All Masters who have evolved through the earth experience, their initiates, lightbearers in incarnation today, and a portion of today's general population, comprising of one to two billion souls in incarnation at a given time, represent the lunar *pitris* stock that is likely to survive the present turmoil, including the floods.

Laggard Populations: Those who will not survive

Earth being in the free will zone of the Universe has been host to countless drop-ins from similar evolutions of other solar systems. Some call them laggards from other evolutions, some call them drop-ins. Smaller populations of laggards date back many millennia when they began incarnating on earth in Third Root-Race or Fourth Root-Race bodies. Their descendents form the core of the Dark Forces that control the earth today.

From the time we passed the halfway point at the bottom of the Fourth Round, no more lunar *pitri* monads were allowed to enter earth:

> ... at this point—and on this Fourth Round in which the human stage will be fully developed—the "Door" into the human kingdom closes; and henceforward the number of "human" Monads, i.e., Monads in the human stage of development, is complete. For the Monads which had not reached the human stage by this point will, owing to the evolution of humanity itself, find themselves so far behind that they will reach the human stage only at the close of the seventh and last Round. They will, therefore, not be men on this chain, but will form the humanity of a future Manvantara and be rewarded by

becoming "Men" on a higher chain altogether, thus receiving their Karmic compensation.[7]

Thus, we can conclude that a pre-destined number of monads are set to evolve on the earth and survive the coming earth changes.

We attribute the unprecedented population explosion over the past few centuries to the large number of non-lunar *pitris* drop-ins. These laggard incarnations account for the lack of homogeneity on earth, distinguishing it from other planets of the solar system with its high level of conflict and disharmony on earth. The Dark Forces have used this influx of incarnations to their advantage, primarily as lackeys, to advance their control over the earth.

Once the earth has undergone its cleansing, the surviving lunar *pitris* monad stock will be given yet another opportunity to regain its path of evolution after suffering millennia of oppression under the laggard stock. This is one of the major landmarks of this present filtering process.

However, it remains a question of choice whether incarnations of the original lunar *pitris* monads will seize this opportunity to right the situation on earth and pursue their evolution as the rightful inhabitants of the earth.

---

[7] Blavatsky, Helena P. *The Secret Doctrine*, Vol. 1, p. 173

Varying Nature of the Surviving Population

Among the surviving incarnations of the lunar *pitris* stock there are differences. From the start, each monad chooses its path and as a result evolves in different ways. Those who follow along the path of the Spiritual Hierarchy eventually evolve into Masters while others who came under the influence of the laggards evolve in the way of darkness until awakened. So we will continue to see the good and the bad, except the bad ones will be hopefully more prone to redemption as they are not irredeemable incarnations.

The Monadic Host may be roughly divided into three great classes as H.P. Blavatsky states:

> The most developed Monads (the Lunar Gods or "Spirits," called, in India, the *Pitris*), whose function it is to pass in the first Round through the whole triple cycle of the mineral, vegetable, and animal kingdoms in their most ethereal, filmy, and rudimentary forms, in order to clothe themselves in, and assimilate, the nature of the newly formed chain. They are those who first reach the human form (if there can be any form in the realm of the almost subjective) on Globe A in the first Round. It is they, therefore, who lead and represent the human element during the second and third Rounds, and finally evolve their shadows at the beginning of the Fourth Round for the second class, or those who come behind them.

Those Monads are the first to reach the human stage during the three and a half Rounds, and to become men.

The laggards; the Monads which are retarded, and which will not reach, by reason of Karmic impediments, the human stage at all during cycle or Round, . . .[8]

The laggards referred to in this citation are the slower lunar *pitris*.   So among the lunar *pitris* there are differences in spiritual development.

As the laggards in a race struggle and plod in their first quarter while the victor darts pass the goal, so, in the race of immortality, some souls outspeed all the rest and reach the end, while their myriad competitors are toiling under the load of matter, close to the starting-point. Some unfortunates fall out entirely, and lose all chance of the prize; some retrace their steps and begin again.[9]

We can thus conclude that just because the majority of the survivors will represent monads of the original stock does not mean we are entering an age where good and bad do not exist.   Earth will continue to entertain a state of duality peopled by a minority of advanced lunar *pitris* monads as well as a vast majority of lunar *pitris*

---

[8]   Blavatsky, H.P. *Collected Writings*, Vol. VII November, 1886.

[9]   Ibid.

monads, all struggling to realize the perfection within their incarnated forms.

The main difference this time is that the majority of the survivors of the coming earth changes will be permitted to resume their evolutionary path unimpeded by the overwhelming power of the Dark Forces. Furthermore, greater homogeneity among the survivors will result in less conflict, and a Golden Age of peace and tranquility can emerge as a workable possibility rather than a pipe dream.

Leaders among the Lunar *Pitri* Monads

Lightbearers represent the Lunar *Pitris* monads who have taken the fast track of initiation in previous incarnations and who have incarnated during this period to lead mankind into a new society. The current government and business leadership will crumble with their respective bureaucratic institutions and leave a void. Lightbearers should emerge to take their place, not necessarily in the same kind of institutions but as spiritual leaders with alternative solutions to life in the new context.

As leaders, they will point the way toward rebalancing the earth following the exit of the Dark Forces. But the vast majority of earth's surviving population will remain on the slow but sure evolutionary path through the Fourth Round.

Conclusion

As we inch our way through the Fourth Round, surviving the great global financial crisis, a World War and regional geological earth changes, the Spiritual Regions will lead the way in shaping the New Age. These regions will first create order out of chaos and set up the transitional society that culls out the good from the old and applies new principles of soul expression. As the rest of the world struggles with the exit of the Dark Forces and the climatic and geological changes, they will look upon the Spiritual Regions for solace, inspiration and a brighter future.

Chapter 3

Healing Earth's Mental Body

Underlying the battle taking place on the earth plane is an ongoing transmutation of matter that is healing the mental bodies of both humanity and the earth itself. In Chapter 1 we briefly summarized the diseased condition of the world today and explained how it has been able to persist because of the preponderant role of the Dark Forces which have manipulated the emotional body of mankind through the astral plane. An overall healing of this condition is taking place due to the very nature of matter.

Even during the darkest days of the transition into the New Age, mankind will continue to evolve, for as the Master Kuthumi suggests in the quote below, matter remains indestructible and exists to change forms, combinations and properties over evolutionary time.

Matter we know to be eternal, i.e. having had no beginning (a) because matter is Nature herself (b) because that which cannot annihilate itself and is indestructible exists necessarily—and therefore it could not begin to be, nor can it cease to be (c) because the accumulated experience of countless ages, and that of exact science show to us matter (or nature) acting by her own peculiar energy, of which not an atom is ever in an absolute state of rest, and therefore it must have always existed, i.e., its materials ever changing form, combinations and properties, but its principles or elements being absolutely indestructible.

. . . we believe in MATTER alone, in matter as visible nature and matter in its invisibility as the invisible omnipresent omnipotent Proteus with its unceasing motion which is its life, and which nature draws from herself since she is the great whole outside of which nothing can exist.[10] *(Italics added)*

The particular state of concrete matter which we know as our third dimensional world is and has always been in flux, changing "form, combinations and properties".   The big difference during this period is the speed in which this flux or transmutation process is taking place under acceleration.

Cosmic Law of Destruction

Transmutation in this particular period is coloured by the Cosmic Law of Destruction.   For many esoteric students, destruction goes against everything they have studied in the New Age teachings which have only

---

[10] Sinnett, A.P., *The Mahatma Letters*,   Letter no. 10 written by the Master Kuthumi, circa 1881, Pasadena: Theosophical University Press, 1992, p. 56.

presented the one-sided "feel good" spirituality. But as we mentioned in the previous chapters, the nature of the creation of the universe is cyclical, and each cycle waxes and wanes. Destruction takes place in the waning stage of a cycle before a new cycle can begin. The old must be discarded and transmuted into a different form. Therefore, much of the transmutation taking place today will look like destruction, but behind the destruction is the phoenix that will rise again.

Transmuting the Concrete Form

During the past centuries the challenge facing the concrete form of the Fifth Root-Race has been to express the intelligence and light of the soul through concrete matter. The enduring ancient Egyptian pyramids, such massive symbols of dense matter, are shaped to point the way upward and to a lighter form.

Detachment from Dense Matter

The massive upheavals of the Twentieth Century, which included countless regional wars and two great World Wars, have not only killed millions but uprooted and displaced billions. This process continues up to today.

On December 26, 2004 a tsunami swept through South Asia and displaced an estimated 1.0 million persons. Later in the summer of 2005, Hurricane Katrina slammed into New Orleans and displaced more than one million persons. These are only two of the most famous flood events but countless floods and population displacements have already taken place without media coverage.[11] These events warn of what is to happen in greater frequency in the years to come. The increasing geological changes and the chaos that result in massive population displacements will challenge humanity's attachment to their material existence.

The collapse of the financial and economic systems and the ensuing economic depression are also signals to humanity to take stock of what they really need to exist on this earth. These major factors—economic collapse, wars and earth changes-- will cause mankind to detach from its material possessions, keeping what is necessary and discarding what does not serve.

Changing of the Racial Stock

The changing of the racial stock goes in tandem with the general transmutation of the earth into a less dense physical planet. During the next five decades we will witness the continued entry of two generations of the new racial stock. The very concrete Fifth Root-Race stock will gradually give way to the lighter material bodies of the incoming Sixth Root-Race. Those in Fifth Root-Race bodies today presently will most likely choose Sixth Root-Race bodies for future reincarnations, a move from the concrete to the lighter form.

---

[11] For a listing of floods around the world since 1985, go to the Dartmouth Flood Observatory flood archives: http://www.dartmouth.edu/~floods/Archives/index.html

Accelerated Transmutation

As stated above, even dense matter of which both earth and its inhabitants are comprised is always in a state of constant flux, but what makes this period even more remarkable is the rapidity of this transmutation process due to acceleration.

Transmutation will gradually steer mankind back onto the path of evolution as mankind adjusts to the incoming accelerated energies. If one's present vehicle cannot adapt to acceleration, it will just perish and reincarnate in a more suitable form, probably in a Sixth Root-Race body, or it may come back in a more advanced form of a Fifth Root-Race body, as the overlapping of the two Root-Races will continue for some time.

Fifth Root-Race incarnations today can make a conscious determination to adjust to the higher vibrations of acceleration. Many of these incarnations wear vehicles of the seventh or last *sub-race* of the Fifth Root-Race and have incarnated to assure the transition from the present civilisation to the New Age. Their knowledge of the good and bad of the present civilization will enable mankind to rebuild our civilization based on maintaining the good from our present civilization and laying the foundations for humanity's progression toward eventual life in the New Age or Fourth Dimension. Their presence, especially early lightbearers who have chosen this type of vehicle, is vital for the transition.

Nonetheless, they will be subjected to the higher vibrations as everyone else, and through meditation they can adjust their vibrations and adapt to the ramping up of energies. This is because being of the last sub-race of the Fifth Root-Race, their body equipment shares some similar characteristics to the incoming Sixth Root-Race incarnations. As they adjust to the higher vibrations, they will experience a loss of weight density, the ability to see etherically and a greater openness to the other dimensions.

In line with the Cosmic Law of Destruction, acceleration also filters out "all that does not serve mankind" in a regime of money, sensual gratification based on mankind's bestial instincts and warmongering. However, cosmic forces will prove to be more compelling. Transmutation will take place whether the Dark Force elements want it or not.

So three factors contribute to the transmutation of the concrete form into a lighter one: 1) the Cosmic Law of Destruction at the end of this cycle and its process of detachment from material assets, 2) the change of the root-race stock, and 3) an acceleration of all atoms that comprise all vibrational levels of matter.

Healing of the Mental Body: A Special Focus

Great Cosmic Minds that form the extension of the Spiritual Hierarchy above and beyond the planet earth are concentrating on healing the mental bodies of the earth and its inhabitants, mankind. They have noted that a great healing of the earth's mental plane as well as the mental bodies of mankind is needed after aeons of misuse by the forces of darkness.

These Great Cosmic Minds decided that the best way to foster this healing was to make everything move faster, i.e. to accelerate the transmutation of matter at all levels with special focus during this fifty-year period on the healing of the lower mental body. This healing is necessary in order to prepare earth and mankind for its entry into the New Age or Fourth Dimension when mind will dominate the emotions.

The mental body is the generator of all thought-forms that eventually take form in dense matter. If it does not function in line with the Divine Plan, mankind cannot advance in the evolutionary process. Over the past centuries, the mass consciousness which forms the general mental material of earth and its inhabitants has been warped and twisted to serve the ends of the Dark Forces. The "every man for himself" syndrome characterizes the major thought patterns that permeate thinking on the earth from the child in the playground to the interactions between nations.

As the accelerated transmutation of matter takes place, it will clear out the astral and emotional blockages that have stymied the functioning and development of the mental body. It will increase the vibrations in the lower mental plane and bodies which make up the concrete intellect and expose hidden machinations, criminal actions, false reasoning, sophism, fictions, untruths and fantasies that are the backbone of the Dark Forces regime today. The speed-up of mental matter will lift thought-forms out of the fog of materialism and selfishness and start a conscious healing of the mental body.

Trends toward Earth's Mental Healing: The 4 D's

The trends toward earth's mental healing will be: 1) de-sensualization, 2) de-militarization, 3) de-politization, and 4) de-monetarization. All represent what needs to be purged from the lower mental bodies of earth and mankind.

De-sensualization

Many elements of our life have been "sensualized" in order to create a binding desire for life in the dense physical. The lower mental intellect has created marketing strategies that use the "sexual hook" in their publicity to sell goods and services.   The "sensual hook" determines what one wears, how one talks, what one eats or listens to, how one dresses and with what perfume to wear, how one coifs, etc.   Many spend their lives acting out advertising images projected upon them.

The "sensual hook" is also used to promote addictions, not only to sex, but to tobacco and marijuana smoking, alcohol, drugs and other obsessive behaviour. "Feeling good" physically, even for a moment, becomes the ultimate goal in life.   In addition, addictions open the person up to entity possession which exacerbates the addiction.

The Dark Forces know that sex is the easiest hook they can use to tie the human personality to its bestial instincts and thwart mankind's evolution. But as acceleration proceeds, the whole atomic structure of the earth plane will accelerate, and the human body will either adapt and move upward and beyond the reach of the "sensual hook" or expire. At that point the "sensual hook" will no longer have any effect.

Acceleration passes down through the mental plane, then through the astral, etheric and finally the physical plane. As it sweeps through the mental plane, the mental bodies in most people will become more activated and stirred with the wisdom of higher mental matter. Some will not be able to handle the activation and will turn insane or expire. Those who survive the acceleration of mental matter will do so only if the mental body is activated enough to take cognizance that it must control astral extremes.

With a more activated mental body, people will reach a point where they will be able to think themselves out of addictions and self-abusive behaviour. The result will be better health and longevity in a cleaner less polluted world. In fact, living to be over 100 years old may become quite commonplace again.

Demilitarization

Those who create war for profit and are anchored in the lower mental and astral bodies will be summarily wiped out through acceleration. Demilitarization will result from the devastating defeat of the Dark Forces in their planned World War and will take place when the enormous and secretive war machines of the Dark Forces are exposed and destroyed. There will no longer exist "war for profit," and the money and effort expended on this dead-end activity will be directed to peaceful benefits to humanity. The long held dream "from swords into ploughshares" will become a reality as determined lightbearers holding key positions around the world start a true process of dismantling and destroying the war machinery.

The demilitarization of the earth will lead to the revamping of international organizations such as the United Nations and its affiliates as well as the breakdown of the sovereign nation-state. It is the principle of the sovereign nation-state that has perpetuated national war machines. The United Nations was built upon the recognition of national sovereignty, where nations are essentially free to do as they please. This is just the way the Dark Forces wanted it, for all they needed to do was to hijack a nation, use its resources to make war and invoke the principle of national sovereignty to protect it from counteractions. The United Nations has thus failed to achieve anything near world peace as a result.

As we move into the New Age, a world without borders is the goal of the Spiritual Hierarchy, and this is not the new world order about which conspiracies talk. It will be a new world order based on the elaboration and implementation of the Divine Plan. It will be comprised of various groups around the world that represent the varied aspects of that Plan. A multitude of groups borne out of the Cosmic Laws of Attraction and Cohesion will manifest group soul plans which will honeycomb together in a new world organization that is committed to implanting the Divine Plan. So with demilitarization will come at long last, "On earth, peace and goodwill toward men."

De-monetarization

The filtering process replaces lower vibrating matter with the higher. The effect is to throw the world's central banks and their control over the fabrication of paper money into disarray as low vibratory matter is transmuted into a higher form. The central banking system will die on the vine. This transmutation will also undermine the monetary basis of the arms and military industries, the energy industries, global corporations, and the worldwide media.

Out of the financial crisis, the world will finally lose confidence in and reject paper fiat currencies, for the Dark Forces and their government counterparts have used this sham money to steal value from each individual's pocket. The veil is already lifting on the cozy complicity of the governmental and banking worlds, and their ability to dupe the public will evaporate. The crash of the banking system will ultimately take down the whole ignominious system of taxation in all countries and thus reduce governments to their knees and ultimately to a general and significant reduction in functions and power and finally their disappearance.

Mankind will pass through a period where barter will serve as the chief means of exchange. This temporary means of exchange will enable mankind to relearn the true value of things. During this time, gold will come out of hiding, and the world will relearn how to augment the efficiency of barter with gold, a saner and divine medium of exchange. Gold's universal recognition of value will serve as yet another stabilizing element in the exchanges of goods and services during the coming period of earth changes.

In the Spiritual Regions morality toward money will change as supply and demand come into balance, and this long-sought-after goal will further spread to the general populations of earth, provided selfishness can also be conquered. The current economic structure is based on a constant state of shortage or lack. In fact economics, as an academic discipline, is based on the premise of scarcity, and this is drummed into the minds of students and the public as a god-given truth.

Balancing supply and demand will manifest as the haves will give to the have-nots. Hopefully by 2050 -2060 a major redistribution of wealth will have occurred, levelling the great gap between the rich and poor in accordance with the Divine Plan. This is not an unattainable dream in the universe, for it exists everywhere in the Universe, except on earth.

This equilibrium of supply and demand will be first demonstrated in the Spiritual Regions which will master sane practices of production and exchange, augmented, if needed, by the precipitation of goods to re-balance any disparities between supply and demand.

Depolitization

It is said that politics boils down to jockeying and negotiating the distribution of wealth among the people. It is a process of who gets what. There will come a public realization that national governments and international bureaucracies seek only to satisfy their own interests and are probably the worst arbiters of society's goods ever invented. They have always served themselves first before the needs of the people and were never created to function as the true arbiters of wealth. This realization will become starker as more corruption is exposed and these organizations fail to come to the rescue of their citizens in times of great need, especially in catastrophic earth changes.

Mankind will realize the inherent parasitic nature of bureaucracies and how they serve a class of politicians and public servants, who in the name of the public good, actually serve the Dark Forces. The tumultuous events that start with the worldwide financial crisis and lead into the geological earth changes will rend this veil. Over the next generation these organizations will gradually die out, representing the last ball and chain on the mass consciousness to be eliminated.

The media, instead of functioning as a propaganda arm of the governments and politicians, will depoliticize events as it reports more and more positive aspects of people and how people are helping other people. This will not be the "feel good" spin that the Dark Forces use to dupe the public. News will instead sensitize the public to the plight of their brethren and tell what it takes to help one's neighbour. This is true planetary progression – the whole planet progresses once people understand that whatever is on earth is for the use of all mankind. Everything is shared; everything is distributed correctly. And this is a mental realization, not an emotional one.

So these four broad trends of the transmutation of matter---de-sensualization, de-militarization, de-monetization and de-politization—are part of the coming liberation of the mass consciousness, the mental healing that will take place over the next fifty years.

Soul Expression Resumes

As the transmutation from denser to lighter matter takes place, mankind will resume the earthly lesson of allowing the light and intelligence of the soul to manifest through the physical body—a goal that has eluded mankind for thousands of years. With the Dark Force elements virtually eliminated, mankind must play "catch up" during this five decade period.

Even though the formula for soul expression as set forth in the sacred sutras of Patanjali has been put on the back burner, it remains valid and practicable. Whether soul liberation among the surviving masses can take place in such a short time remains to seen, but the Spiritual Hierarchy's never ending optimism and great hope for mankind never cease.

The Transmutation Process Underlies All Change

As the soul manifests more and more clearly through the physical body, the body rises in vibrations and thus gains abilities to perceive matter in its proper context, i.e. as just another form of the same energy or substance that makes up the universe. This is what Helena P. Blavatsky termed as the ability to perceive the permeability of matter. In other words, matter is not as solid as we conceive of it today, and when this realization comes to light, the spiritual seeker is able to demonstrate dominion over dense matter, manifesting needs, healing the sick and even overcoming death.

Emotions come under Mental Control

Emotions tie mankind to dense matter because they necessarily operate from the lower chakras. The Dark Forces control mankind through its emotions-- its fears, desires, sexual promiscuity, the whole gamut of addictions and psychological maladies—and they use black magic, propaganda and disinformation to maintain their grip on mankind.

As accelerated energies filter down from our higher vehicles, they also activate the upper mental body to receive and transmit the impulses of soul to the physical personality. By this very activation, the astral or emotional body comes more under the control of the mental body. This will help temper the mankind's usual emotive responses with more reasoning and thought.

As individual self-control increases, "the herd mentality" which the Dark Forces have capitalized upon will fade out. Even today the rising level of mental discernment is making it more difficult for governments to spin the truth by tapping into fear and or emotional excitement. This is a start of mass scepticism, a sign that the mental is beginning to take over. But the key to getting to this stage is individual self-control of the emotions and the tempering of mass emotional responses.

Etheric Vision and Truthfulness

In the next two to three decades—a short time in evolutionary terms—we can expect the general population to re-acquire etheric vision and practice more telepathic communication.   These two go hand in hand.

Etheric vision is the ability of the physical eye to see etheric matter, the first level of invisible matter beyond the physical.   To the physical eye, this dimension of matter is normally invisible.   But those who do possess etheric vision can see auras, fairies, etheric bodies of "dead" people, energy fields encasing animate or inanimate objects--all with the physical eye.   However, given the present condition of material numbness, the general population has suppressed this ability.   Those who gravitate toward the Spiritual Regions will as a matter of course re-acquire this ability.

Etheric vision is already widespread among lightbearers.   The accelerated transmutation of matter will play a large part in stimulating the brain cells to pick up the whole range of what the physical eye is capable of seeing.   When etheric vision becomes prevalent in the population, this should signal that the transmutation from the concrete to the lighter is taking hold.

The re-acquisition of etheric vision will bring about an age of truth.   The dense body and brain provide very good hiding places for lies and deception. But the etheric body reacts inharmoniously to lies or grey area untruths. Changes in visible energy patterns can betray hidden thoughts and actions and bring them to the surface. Thus, etheric vision will enable us to see this disharmony of energies, expose spin and lies and give mankind a better perception of truthfulness.

As the society transits through the next five decades, there will be more upheavals on all levels of society as deep-seated lies rise to the surface. People will blurt out deeply held secrets and expose the darker, their secretive side. This is happening today in its grosser forms e.g. politics but will permeate human society until all is flushed out for the better.

The incoming Sixth Root Race incarnations naturally possess etheric vision, which is currently being suppressed as "weird". As young and adult Sixth Root-Race members realize that this ability is to be enhanced rather than suppressed, etheric vision will become more widespread and accepted. The media shall talk of etheric vision and the exercises that will enhance it. These include certain meditation techniques and concentration exercises. So in a world of increasing enhanced "seeing", lies will decrease, and truthfulness will again become a virtue. Another veil of dense concrete matter will have been pierced.

Telepathic Communication

Telepathic communication between two individuals is already widespread. Thoughts and messages pass through the byways of the lower etheric sub-planes and are evidence that we are already dealing to a certain extent with the next dimension, the Fourth. For example, just thinking of someone can often result in contact through email or a telephone call. Telepathic communications between spouses and between mother and child are quite commonplace.

As acceleration clears the astral haze with the downfall of the Dark Forces, the ability to transfer more complex information telepathically will increase. Wireless technology is a precursor of what we will be able to transmit through telepathy. At the same time, and most importantly, this ability, like etheric vision, enhances one's perception of the truth and provides no hiding place for untruth.

In Volume 1, we showed how the Dark Forces have used flickering rays emitted from the television set to numb the brains of the world's populations. Those who have consciously freed themselves of this catatonic stupor will find that their brains will be able to reactivate etheric vision and the ability to communicate telepathically, provided damage from years of exposure to the television has not impaired their abilities permanently.

As these two abilities return to the surface, the reconstruction efforts in the Spiritual Regions will benefit. The sifting of the good and bad will come under even heavier scrutiny, and hiding lies and untruths in dense matter will no longer be possible.

Structural Deterioration and Collapse

As these etheric abilities begin to manifest, not only will the very foundations of material physics be put to question, but mankind will begin to defy established limitations and begin to dominate the world of matter, in other words, understanding the permeability of matter. All material forms—cars, houses, roads, bridges, buildings, trains, airplanes—have a calculated term of amortization. But with increasing acceleration, rapid amortization of these material forms will surprise many engineers. Even the most enduring structures the world cherishes will show signs of more rapid deterioration.

We are already witnessing the deterioration of roads and bridges built only within the last 50 years, and untimely or unexpected collapses of these structures will become more frequent. New, lighter materials are already coming into use and replacing the steel, bricks, mortar and concrete era.

So as acceleration continues to ramp up, our physicists and scientists will have to take another look at Mr. Newton's laws. Even today signs of matter's permeability are taken for granted: wireless technologies are now capable of penetrating solid structures. Medical technologies such as MRI machines can see through the physical body. Understanding the permeability of matter will have a profound effect on our whole society.

As part of mental healing, acceleration will call to question all the theories of physics governing engineering, electricity, and electronics, and add more empirical proof of matter's permeability. Scientists of physics and chemistry will again retrace some of the principles of ancient esoteric alchemy—a product of man's former etheric form of a bygone era.

A major challenge to the current laws of physics will come again from the occult world. The precipitation of forms or apports in the trans-physical séances of the past Spiritualist Movement afforded a peek into a new era. Yet scientists have shied away from explaining these phenomena by brushing them aside as the work of tricksters and frauds. Yet, even the major religions of the world admit that spiritual adepts have been able to manifest objects and food, seemingly out of nowhere. The Master Jesus so demonstrated this ability 2000 years ago by feeding the masses with a few loaves and fishes.

When this ability to manifest becomes more and more demonstrable and commonplace, it will open up a new world of thinking that involves the participation of another kingdom, the Deva or Elemental Kingdom, in our existence. Needless to say, that gradual appearance of form building that does not require the factory production line, agricultural fields, or hammer and nails, will revolutionize science's assumptions and the laws of physics. So in the next fifty years, this method of form building will no longer be restricted to the spiritual séance or cave yogis; it will take place on such a frequent and universal scale that the scientific community will have to recognize it as scientific material—and this will be possible with the influx of the Sixth Root-Race.

At first this type of form building will demand the active cooperation of the lightbearers and the Deva Kingdom. It will begin more from wishing or conjuring up clear thought-forms that will result in synchronicities of events or resources coming together to produce the manifestation. Clear thoughts will materialize in a most "miraculous" way, like "wishing upon a star" and having the events unfold.

Later the transforming of thought-forms into observable etheric or physical forms will come under each person's control. But that day is dependent on the individual's spiritual development, the first manifestations of widespread phenomena building likely occurring in the purer atmosphere of the Spiritual Regions.

Organizational Collapse

The collapse of the world's largest and most powerful investment banks, followed by the banking system is yet another example of the kind of organizational collapse that the future will continue to bring. Again, all organisations that do not serve mankind will deteriorate faster and crumble. And this is still part of the ongoing transmutation from the concrete to the lighter form.

Organized religions will suffer as well. Acceleration will churn its way into petrified church and religious structures, roiling their religious concepts and dogmas and emptying out their churches. All forms of religious thought have already been subjected to deterioration for the past 100 years and their empty buildings, temples and churches are a testament to their irrelevance. The crumbling of organized religions will accelerate even further during the next fifty years and the lighter unaligned spirituality will take its place.

Media will Reform

As the Dark Forces lose control of the media, the light forces will take over and begin reporting about the good side of mankind.   Stories will abound about the goodness of individuals and how those with resources share with those who do not have much.   Mankind will realize with the help of the media its essential goodness and this realization will spread around the globe.

Medical Systems Pared Down

Higher vibrations will also call into question the need for much of the invasive, dense and addictive measures our medical systems now force on mankind.   It is a blatant form of bondage.   Tinctures of homeopathy will play a greater role to restore balance in lightened physical bodies.   People outside the medical establishment will invent simple solutions for a range of illnesses that the individual can administer.   The days of the preponderant medical infrastructure, training, medicaments and drugs industries and basically getting rich on people's sorrows and illnesses will gradually draw to an end.   It will start with the simple proposition that the economic depression will bring about: people will not be able to pay for the increasingly outrageous costs of medical care, and the medical structure will have to adapt or disappear.   This is all part of the dismantling of a significant sector of Dark Forces hegemony over humanity.

Expansion of All Disciplines

Both the physical and biological sciences will undergo a necessary upheaval as both the physical body and world around it start to lighten. Research scientists unconsciously experiencing etheric vision and telepathic abilities will probe into ethereal aspects of ALL disciplines as their understanding of matter's permeability deepens.

Psychology

With most people spinning out of control because of acceleration, we should call psychology "damage control." Psychology will hopefully take a leap forward during the next fifty years as the conscious mind itself opens up to other dimensions.

Psychologists will come to realize that many psychological problems attributed to one's struggle in the material life can be more accurately understood as a result the conscious mind's peregrinations in and out of the astral plane. They will further realize how astral entities that attach to human beings can drive a person to carry out insane or quirky actions that he or she would otherwise not do. We cite some of mass murderers who are "normal" until they are "seized by the devil."

Much abnormal and insane behaviour has its origin in these astral influences rather than in traditional psychological or medical causes. We also see a connection between astral attachments and symptoms such as mental depression, obsessive behaviour, addictions to alcohol and drugs, and the like. When these astral attachments are removed, this type of behaviour is rectified. Until the effects of astral attachments are recognized by the psychology profession, psychological problems will continue to be attributed to the wrong cause.

The best combination would be a trained psychologist who has developed etheric vision or who wears a Sixth Root-Race body. Etheric vision will enable the counselling professions to see a connection between astral attachments and symptoms such as mental depression, obsessive behaviour, addictions to alcohol and drugs, and the like.

The study of psychology will flow along with the whole process of the transmutation of matter or like any of the other disciplines, it will be left behind in evolution's dust.

Biological Sciences

In the biological sciences, the implications of matter's transmutation are grand, for almost all our medical and traditional practices, good and bad, about diet, nutrition and health come from the basic scientific assumptions of these sciences. Much of mankind's efforts to live each day are taken up by what we eat and how we care for our physical bodies. In the near future, the speed of bodily functions will increase in tandem with the increased velocity of the atoms in each cell of the body vehicle,

Energy conversion will be the object of much study and re-evaluation. With acceleration, our bestial instincts to prey on the other kingdoms for sustenance will gradually disappear. In its place we will enter a period where each kingdom is rightfully sustained by direct pranic intake rather than the conversion method or digestion of breaking down foods for energy. When we reach the stage where ingestion of pranic energy suffices to sustain the inhabitants of all kingdoms, we will have reached a major stage of transmutation. In the meantime, people will gradually learn to eat less and absorb prana more: and what they eat will be of lighter vegetable materials rather than heavy flesh regimes.

Our diets today differ quite a lot from that which was eaten 100 years ago. The body's tolerance of the toxins contained in our common foods and which is manifested by widespread obesity and other diseases not common years ago, will naturally give way to intolerance. Higher vibrational bodies will naturally reject heavy flesh-based foods, and eat plants of a higher vibration as the earth changes. We will observe these changes first in the Spiritual Regions.

Agriculture

Profound changes in agriculture will emerge when plant genetic materials that exist under the current ice caps come into the hands of the agriculturalist. This plant matter has been preserved for centuries for the coming of this era. So from this new flora will emerge new ways of sustaining an accelerated body based on advanced vegetarian principles. This will be the last step of material ingestion and will eventually lead to the ingestion of prana for energy rather than food prepared from plant or animal substances.

Revolution of the Educational Systems

Acceleration will also affect greatly the educational systems—the inadaptive ones will be the Fifth Root-Race while the Sixth Root-Race will flourish in the heightened vibrations. To keep up with them will be a problem if one approaches education from the traditional point of view. The early incarnations of the Sixth Root-Race have already been implanted as future educators and will know how to educate children of the Sixth Root-Race. (See Chapter 2)

Resurgence of Astrology

At one point in history, astrology became of threat to the Dark Forces because of its ability to gauge personality and thus reveal motivations and intentions. In addition it could predict timing cycles in line with the cosmic Law of Periodicity. However, in a stroke of hypocrisy, the Science of Astrology was shunted to the sidelines of mainstream scientifically based knowledge and declared unscientific while the Dark Forces continued to delve deep into this science for information about cycles in order to control the earth. In fact, civilisation failed to look upon astrology as a great gift from the Spiritual Hierarchy that was meant to help mankind flourish in dense matter.

During the next fifty years, we will witness a surprising change in the way humans perceive our planet and stars, especially in the West. As we continue to exist in ever higher vibrations, we will become more sensitive to the influences of the stars and planets, and thus astrology as we know it today will have to be rewritten. Not that all will change, but the subtler and more accurate descriptions of the planets (these Great Souls) and their influence on the state of worldly affairs will become more evident.

One of the main advantages of astrology is timing. Mankind will learn to subordinate time to the mind and thus gain the ability to predict and overcome the vagaries of time as an evolved knowledge of astrology takes root in the educational system. Astrology will return to its place of pre-eminence, first in the Spiritual Regions, where children will learn this science from a very young age and learn to steer their lives in line with cosmic trends and forces.

As a result, the directionless individual in society should be the exception.

Opening of the Human Consciousness

As the above trends take root, human thought will be freed at last from the fetters of the Dark Forces regime. Mankind will come to realize how confined and restricted the regime of the Dark Forces had been and hopefully a conscious realization will set in to prevent any repeat of such a regime in the future.

As we flow with the transmutation of matter at this stage, we will spend much time re-evaluating the good and the bad of our past civilization and literally reach for the stars in terms of human creativity.

The Master St. Germain said, "The benefits of the karmic redressing known as the 'Armageddon' will be felt for centuries and centuries to come." The fall of the Dark Forces money and warmongering machine will open opportunities not seen by mankind for centuries, and these opportunities will be defined by the ever changing nature of matter as it evolves to higher vibrations.

Every aspect, every discipline, every field of endeavour has a higher dimension. It is the new frontier to be explored and is driven by the eternal search for the truth. Even carpentry and plumbing, these two stalwarts of the builder trade, have a higher dimension. So the fields of discovery are infinite.

During the Twentieth-first Century a broad range of scientific and technological discoveries will come to light, especially in the Spiritual Regions. It is the potential that has always existed in mankind, that godhead that stands behind all human endeavours that will rush to the surface as part of St. Germain's program of soul liberation.

"Now we begin the upward climb", the design of ascension built into the solid rock structure of the pyramid, pointing to the apex. Keeping a watchful eye over the above indicators will give us an idea of how we are being prepared to take our first steps into the Fourth Dimension.

Chapter 4

First Steps into the Fourth Dimension

. . . we are now well into the second half of the 4th Round, and the 5th Race has discovered a fourth state of matter and a 4th "dimension of space". Master Kuthumi[12]

Many today wonder where all the turmoil and earth changes are leading us. The answer is that with the transmutation from the concrete to lighter forms, we are taking the first steps into the Fourth Dimension as part of the Divine Plan. These initial steps of transmutation involve the healing of the mental body of both earth and its inhabitants before they can attain entry into the next dimension. The ultimate goal is for all of mankind to be functioning in the Fourth Dimension by the end of the Fourth Round. Today's crumbling of the financial and economic system marks the first step in a millennial

---

[12] A handwritten comment under the name of "E.O." (Eminent Occultist) or the Master Kuthumi to the translator (Mr. A. O. Hume) in his English version of the French *The Paradoxes of the Highest Science* by French mystic and occultist Eliphas Levi, 1883.

journey into the next dimension, and the implications therein are quite profound.

In the above quote, the Master Kuthumi states that the Fifth Root-Race has already discovered the fourth state of matter or the 4th Dimension in space. Let us first see what the Fifth Root-Race has been able to uncover about the Fourth Dimension.

Early Notions of the Fourth Dimension

Delving into the Fourth Dimension has been a fairly modern, western notion, although the great yogis of India and Tibet have known and experienced it firsthand without defining it as such. Over the past two centuries, western philosophers and scientists have intuitively discerned that there could be another dimension beyond our five senses. Immanuel Kant, 18th Century German philosopher, posited:

> A science of these kinds of possible space would undoubtedly be the highest enterprise which a finite understanding could undertake in the field of geometry. . . . If it is possible there could be regions with other dimensions, it is very likely that God has somewhere brought them into being.[13]

---

[13] Quoted in Rucker, Rudy, *The Fourth Dimension, A Guided Tour of the Higher Universes,* Houghton Mifflin; Reprint edition (Aug 14 1985)

An Experiment in Transcendental Physics

In the late 1870's, Professor Johan Gael Friedrich Zollner of Leipzig, Germany, an eminent astronomer, physicists, and philosopher, ventured outside the "box" of scientific and mathematical thinking in order to prove the existence of a Fourth Dimension. He was also a metaphysician and had long surmised that besides length, breadth, and thickness, there might be a fourth dimension of space. If this were so, he surmised, then there would be another world of being, distinct from our three-dimensional world, with its own inhabitants fitted to its four-dimensional laws and conditions, as we are to ours in the Third Dimensions. He was not the originator of this theory; Kant, and, later Gauss, the metaphysical geometer, had spoken of this possibility earlier.

With the aid of Dr. Henry Slade, an American spiritual medium, Professor Zollner created a series of experiments that would prove his hunch as well as convince his colleagues of the existence of the Fourth Dimension.

Professor Zollner started with the proposition that there exists a world of four dimensions with four-dimensional inhabitants. These latter ought to be able to perform the simple experiment of tying hard knots in an endless cord, for the fourth property of matter—the Fourth Dimension of space—must be permeability.

He and Dr. Slade he took a cord, tied the two ends together, sealed them with wax and then stamped it with his own signet. The Professor sat next to Dr. Slade at a table in broad daylight, their four hands laid upon the table, Slade's feet in sight, and the endless cord with the sealed end lying on the table under the Professor's thumbs. The loop hung down and rested upon his lap. It was the first time Dr. Slade had heard of such an experiment, and no one had tried it with any other medium. In a few seconds the Professor felt a slight motion of the cord—which no one was touching—and upon looking, found to his surprise and joy that his wish had been granted: only, instead of one knot, four had been tied in his cord![14]

Both devised other experiments for their sceptical audiences. One demonstrated that the contents of a sealed chest could be removed by these fourth dimensional entities without breaking the seal.

To a scientific mind like his, this result, though infinitely less sensational than hundreds of mediumistic phenomena, was as conclusive and important a proof of the theory of four dimensions, as was the falling of a single apple to Newton in corroborating his immortal theory of gravity. Here was clearly an instance of the

---

[14] *Transcendental Physics.* An account of experimental Investigations, from the Scientific Treatises of Johann Carl Friedrich Zöllner, Professor of Physical Astronomy at the University of Leipzig; Mem. Royal Saxon Soc. of Sciences, etc., etc., translated from German, with a Preface and Appendices, by Charles Carleton Massey, of Lincoln's Inn, Barrister-at-Law (Vice-President of the Theosophical Society) as recounted in *The Theosophist*, Vol. II, No. 5, February, 1881, pp. 95-97

passage of matter through matter, in short, the cornerstone of a whole system of cosmic philosophy.

The publication of these experiments created an intense interest as well as furor and derision throughout the world of science. Professor Zollner was accused of being "taken in" by Dr. Slade, who in turn was attacked as being merely a magician and confidence man. Only early Theosophists, including H.P. Blavatsky, praised him.

The property which we have here clumsily designated as a "fourth" dimension of space is known throughout the whole East by appropriate and specific terms among not only scholars but the very "jugglers" who make boys disappear from beneath baskets. If Western scientists would familiarize themselves a little more with the Pythagorean Tetraktys, or even with the algebraical "unknown quantity" in its transcendental meaning, all difficulties in the way of accepting Zollner's hypothesis would disappear.[15]

Later, in the early 1900's C. Howard Hinton set upon a quest to find and define the physical reality of a fourth dimension. Innately conscious of a higher world than our third dimensional one, he was looking for " . . . a world spatially higher than this world, a world which can only be approached through the stocks and stones of it, a world which must be apprehended laboriously, patiently, through the material things of it, the shapes, the

---

[15] *Banner of Light,* Boston, Vol. XLII, April 20,1878

movements, the figures of it."[16] His courageous efforts to reach for that "world spatially higher" through the use of analogy and geometric drawings further hinted that the Fifth Root-Race would indeed discover the existence of a Fourth Dimension, as the Master Kuthumi prophesized.

However, most of the "hardcore" scientific minds of the early 20th Century found it difficult to validate what the spiritualists were witnessing in the séance room daily i.e. speaking to the dead. Refusing to leave their ivory towers in the Third Dimension, they could only think of the Fourth Dimension in terms of mathematics and geometry.

In 1909, Scientific American offered a $500.00 prize for the best essay, "What is the Fourth Dimension?" in 2500 words or less. The contest drew 245 entries from all over the world, and the winner was Lieutenant-Colonel Graham Denby Fitch from the US Corps of Engineers, USA. His background would seem to negate any concession to the spiritualist but surprisingly, he did not dismiss happenings of their séances and was quoted as follows:

> Hyperspace (ed. Fourth Dimension) has been brought somewhat into disrepute because spiritualists have assumed its existence in order to give "a local habitation" to their vagaries. Nevertheless, the possibility of its existence has not yet been shown to be inconsistent with any scientific fact, and the

---

[16] Hinton, C. Howard, *The Fourth Dimension*, New Hampshire: Ayer Company, Publishers, Inc, 1988, p. 3. (Reprint edition)

limitation of space to three dimensions, though probably correct, is therefore purely empirical.[17]

This intense interest among intellectuals, physicists, mathematicians and astronomers corresponded to the zenith of the Fifth Root-Race physical intellectuality that the Master Kuthumi spoke of in the *Mahatma Letters*. Most of the essayists, although steeped in non-Euclidean geometry and mathematics were generous enough to hold the door open to what they called the "spiritist" point of view.

The Sixth Sense or Natural Clairvoyance

All these attempts to define and perceive the Fourth Dimension with the five physical senses were bound to meet with only half success. As the Zollner experiments demonstrated in his use of a spiritual medium, an extra-sensory key was necessary. H.P. Blavatsky stated in *The Secret Doctrine*: that mankind would come to recognize the permeability of matter. Any object that is perceived to be solid is actually made up of millions of atoms, all spinning independently with space in between them. Matter is thus inherently permeable.

Blavatsky states that the only way to prove this permeability is for man to develop a sixth sense or what she calls "normal clairvoyance".

---

[17] Fitch, Graham Denby, "An Elucidation of the Fourth Dimension", part I of his prize-winning essay of the 1909 *Scientific American* essay contest "What is the Fourth Dimension"

. . . it is worthwhile to point out the real significance of the sound but incomplete intuition that has prompted—among Spiritualists and Theosophists, and several great men of Science . . . the use of the modern expression "the fourth dimension of Space." . . . The familiar phrase can only be an abbreviation of the fuller form—the "Fourth dimension of MATTER in Space." But it is an unhappy phrase even thus expanded, because while it is perfectly true that the progress of evolution may be destined to introduce us to new characteristics of matter, those with which we are already familiar are really more numerous than the three dimensions. The faculties, or . . . the characteristics of matter, must clearly bear a direct relation always to the senses of man. Matter has extension, colour, motion (molecular motion), taste, and smell, corresponding to the existing senses of man, and by the time that it fully develops the next characteristic—let us call it for the moment PERMEABILITY—this will correspond to the next sense of man—let us call it "NORMAL CLAIRVOYANCE;" thus, when some bold thinkers have been thirsting for a fourth dimension to explain the passage of matter through matter, and the production of knots upon an endless cord, what they were really in want of, was a sixth characteristic of matter.[18]

So developing that sixth sense beyond our five senses in order to see dense matter through normal clairvoyance

---

[18] Blavatsky, Helena P. *The Secret Doctrine*, Vol. 1 p. 251-52

as permeable is the key to perceiving the Fourth Dimension.

As to those past and current efforts to define and speculate about the Fourth Dimension from the vantage point of the Third Dimensional mindset and senses, using geometry, tetra cubes, computer models etc. the Fourth Dimension will remain elusive although these efforts cannot help but prepare the mass consciousness for something new.

> The three dimensions belong really but to one attribute or characteristic of matter—extension; and popular common sense justly rebels against the idea that under any condition of things there can be more than three of such dimensions as length, breadth, and thickness. These terms, and the term "dimension" itself, all belong to one plane of thought, to one stage of evolution, to one characteristic of matter. . . . But these considerations do not militate in any way against the certainty that in the progress of time—as the faculties of humanity are multiplied—so will the characteristics of matter be multiplied also."[19]

Abilities of the Sixth Sense

The sixth sense or natural clairvoyance is the key for the present and future races to cognize the Fourth Dimension. For many Lightbearers and occultists on the Path, these faculties are already functioning, but for our

---

[19] Ibid., p. 252

purposes, let us concentrate on etheric vision because this is probably the first faculty that will be obvious to most people in the coming decades.

Etheric Vision: the Initial Perception of the Fourth Dimension

Again, etheric vision is the ability of the physical eye to perceive auras and energy fields around objects and forms. This sixth sense marks the beginning of mankind's perception of matter's permeability.

The human eye apparently already sees much more than the brain can cognize. The actual understanding and cognition of this image takes place in the brain after the image has been transmitted from the retina via the optic nerve to the brain and that extra visual ability that etheric vision affords actually takes place in the brain, not in the eye.

The change that enables the brain to cognize the etheric comes as a result of: 1) the ongoing acceleration of energies that increases the molecular activity in the body and brain, creating a more sensitive eye, optic nerve, and brain. 2) the cleansing of the astral haze which follows the expulsion of the Dark Forces during these times of turmoil 3) the cultivation of higher vibrations that comes through the understanding and study of the Ancient Wisdom, and 4) deep and routine meditation that increases soul contact.

The Sixth Sense or Etheric Vision in Fifth and Sixth Root-Races

In the Mahatma Letters, the Master Kuthumi revealed that the current Fifth Root-Race began one million years ago. Like all previous Root-Races, the Fifth Root-Race is comprised of seven sub-races and mankind is destined to experience each cycle of these sub-races. At that time in the 1880's, Kuthumi revealed that the Colonial British and North American populations represented the seventh sub-race of the Fifth Root-Race or the highest point of physical intellectuality of the Fifth Root-Race. That was in the 1880's.

The Master also revealed that when a Root-Race –in this case our Fifth Root-Race – reaches its zenith of physical intellectuality and is "unable to go any higher in its own cycle, its progress towards absolute evil will be arrested . . . by one of such cataclysmic changes; its great civilization destroyed, and all the sub-races of that race will be found going down their respective cycles, after a short period of glory and learning . . . . No mother Race, any more than her sub-races and off-shoots, is allowed by the one Reigning Law to trespass upon the prerogatives of the Race or Sub-race that will follow it; least of all — to encroach upon the knowledge and powers in store for its successor. "Thou shalt not eat of the fruit of Knowledge of Good and Evil of the tree that is growing for thy heirs."[20]

---

[20] Mahatma Letter 93 B, paragraph 5

121

We interpret this statement to mean the following: The Fifth Root-Race has been gradually declining and exiting and reached its zenith at the start of the Twentieth Century. Overlapping the presence of the Fifth Root-Race, the a few souls of the first generation of the Sixth Root-Race began incarnating on earth, as early as the latter half of the 19th Century, perhaps starting 1861 to 1875.[21]

During the past fifty years, many of these precursors of the Sixth Root-Races have incarnated and are endowed with the sixth sense needed to perceive the Fourth Dimension. But because education in the world today is still decidedly a product of Fifth Root-Race thinking, this potential has been suppressed, but will come alive again in the years to come.

We also know that due to acceleration, the sixth sense is also being activated in the seventh sub-race of the Fifth Root-Race. This activation can also be enhanced through meditation and study of the Ancient Wisdom.

Thus the potential of the sixth sense faculty to emerge, that which will enable human beings to begin perceiving the Fourth Dimension, exists quite strongly on the earth today, unbeknownst to most people. In their most visible form, there are many psychic individuals who serve as mediums and psychics but there are many more who have yet to acknowledge this ability.

---

[21] This period corresponds to the planet Neptune passing through Aries then through the rest of the Zodiac signs to where it sits today until 2012 in the sign of Aquarius.

Location of the Fourth Dimension

The illustration below shows diagrammatically the entire etheric plane as it is divided into seven etheric sub-planes. The lowest and densest sub-planes, 7th, 6th, and 5th, represent our Third Dimensional physical world and correspond to the mineral, plant and animal kingdoms respectively. The next level up is the 4th etheric sub-plane where the Fourth Dimension begins and is *invisible* to the common physical eye. This 4th etheric sub-plane is the entry to the Fourth Dimension. All the sub-planes above it, the 3rd, 2nd, and 1st, comprise the finer states of the Fourth Dimension.

The bottom or densest level of the *invisible* fourth dimensional etheric world is the 4th etheric sub-plane and can be cognized progressively by etheric vision. Etheric vision cannot see beyond this level.

Sub-planes	The Etheric Plane
1	Highest Fourth Dimensional sub-plane
2	Middle Fourth Dimensional sub-plane
3	Middle Fourth Dimensional sub-plane
4	Lowest Fourth Dimensional sub-plane
5	Third Dimension Animal Kingdom
6	Third Dimension Plant Kingdom
7	Third Dimension Mineral Kingdom

As we proceed up the third, second and first etheric sub-planes we move into progressively finer and faster vibrating etheric matter which is all invisible to the physical eye, but the mind's third eye in the center of the head, if developed, can cognize life on these higher etheric sub-planes.

Thus the 4th etheric sub-plane is the first step into the invisible half of our etheric world. It is that level which at one time represented mankind's densest physical existence until the so-called "Fall of Adam" produced the dense physical realm. After we have passed through the cleansing process of this transition on earth, the door will again open for humanity to re-enter or reclaim this first level of the Fourth Dimension.

After entering the Fourth Dimension, the upward climb or ascension is in essence our spiritual journey from the 4th etheric sub-plane to the 1st etheric sub-planes. After we have reached the 1st etheric sub-plane, we will have completed the evolutionary journey of the Fourth Round on earth. Earth will then self-destruct and we will enter a major pralaya or rest period after which our same monads will regroup on another planet, probably in refined mental bodies, in what will be the Fifth Round. This is the long range direction of our evolutionary plan; however, our immediate focus in this book is the puny fifty year period that will embark us on this path.

Hints of the Fourth Dimension

In the above experiments, there were hints of living beings already existing in the Fourth Dimension. Once we are able to cognize this dimension, we will share it with other heretofore unseen inhabitants: the elementals or devas and beings of the angelic realm.

In our Third Dimension, clairvoyants can already observe the workings of this Deva Kingdom. So as people rediscover nature and her bounty without the veil that the Dark Forces have cast over it, they will also encounter this other kingdom and gradually learn to integrate themselves into the life streams of these beings, in much the same way we have learned to live with our pet animals.

With the spread of etheric vision, physical sightings of our deva friends will become more and more frequent. It should start by catching a movement in the corner of one's eye. Dreams of this dimension may become more and more real. Things may disappear only to reappear where they were put in the first place. There is a movement in the bedroom or the house cat chases something invisible. Such "strange" happenings will multiply until the deva kingdom becomes more boldly visible. The 6th Root-Race will focus in on this kingdom and the more advanced sub-races of the 5th Root-Race will learn to interact with this deva kingdom as well.

This gradual integration into the Fourth Dimensions will come primarily with a more harmonious integration with nature. Incredible innovations of technology will come out of the respect for nature and will begin to touch the hem of the Fourth Dimension of most things. For example, energy (oil, petroleum) has a Fourth Dimensional aspect, and that is free energy. This concept made its debut in the Tesla experiments at the turn of the century only to be brutally suppressed. Free energy will finally dominate the energy field, for as can be seen-- coal, oil, wood—are the dense captors of that same energy. The freeing of this energy from the captors is to see energy in its Fourth Dimensional terms.

Forces of Production and Form-Building Re-defined

We will also begin to see and understand the ongoing process of creation as we learn to observe builder devas or elementals form building. We will be able to contrast how people were enslaved in factories of production in the material regime. The whole regime of factory/industrial production will eventually give way to the "real" builders.

The creative process of visualizing what we need in order to carry out the Divine Plan sets in motion a chain reaction of deva activity. Mankind will learn how to cooperate with this creative activity in order to manifest all that will serve good. The re-demonstration of some of the "miracles" that the Master Jesus performed, such as multiplying loaves and fishes to feed the masses will no longer strike awe in people but be most commonplace in life on the Fourth Dimension.

The Way into the Fourth Dimension

It is either by individual effort on the Path of Initiation or through the successive generations of Sixth Root-Race vehicles that the human mind will evolve to the point of lifting itself into the Fourth Dimension. We know that great yogis and occultists have advanced into the Fourth Dimension through the Path of Initiation. This path is always available to those who choose to advance spiritually.

For the greater population of earth, the birth-death cycles will also eventually carry them into the Fourth Dimension but at a slower pace. New incarnations will enter the earth in   Sixth Root-Race vehicles that will be increasingly able to see and exist in the Fourth Dimension.

Human evolution demands the ever-liberation of the soul and in the years to come the soul will express itself through the ever-evolving etheric racial stock that is carrying mankind into the Fourth Dimension. Today, the soul struggles to express itself as best it can through our dense physical bodies. Once our dense physical bodies give way to our etheric body, we will be able to operate on the 4th etheric sub-plane. This etheric body is what pundits of the New Age Movement call the light body.

Through the dense physical body the soul merely finds a speck of an opening to shine through, but through the etheric body, it will shine through to a greater degree, thus creating a whole new universe of possibilities in form. The lighter etheric matter affords the soul a greater window of expression. It is like clear glass versus translucent glass.

There are vast lessons to be learned and life to be experienced on the etheric plane. We can look forward to this prospect without fear. In essence, we are re-visiting our lives on that plane, for before we devolved into dense physical matter, we lived on this plane. Since then, our souls have experienced millions of years of involution and journeyed through some of the densest matter in the universe trying to express intelligence through dense matter. We are now returning to the etheric plane, hopefully all the wiser and with a greater sense of dominion. Lessons learned previously through dense matter will carry over to the etheric. We will be much like the blind person who has learned to grope through life using other senses and who gradually opens up to normal vision.

When the earth has met the fundamental conditions of rebalancing, we will all stand at the threshold of this new dimension. The long trek through dense matter will have shown us that no matter what, the soul will find a way to shine through any vehicle of expression.

Guidance from the Brotherhood of Light

New teachings from the Brotherhood of Light will begin to appear over the next decades. These teachings will mark the way for mankind to undertake its journey into the Fourth Dimension and will add to the Ancient Wisdom we have learned up to now. An avatar, the World Teacher, in whatever form the Spiritual Hierarchy deems suitable, will again set forth teachings that will help mankind find its way into this new dimension, just as Buddha and Jesus the Christ set the spiritual standards for the Piscean era.

As usual mankind is not being sent blindfolded into a new dimension, and the seeker of truth will receive the gentle hand of guidance from their age-old friends of the Brotherhood.

Chapter 5

Seeding the Mass Consciousness

A few months after the "attack" on the twin towers in New York on September 11, 2001, the Sanctus Germanus website published an opinion calling the incident "the greatest act of treason" committed in the USA. The implication of this statement was that the perpetrators of this disaster came from within the US and not from some far off cave in Afghanistan. Today, a decade after this incident, it is widely known among millions around the world that 9/11 came from within and not at all from what has been in the world press.

Expert structural and demolition engineers from around the world have concluded that the collapse of the Twin Towers resulted from a careful and wilful demolition rather than the airliner attack that was portrayed so dramatically on the world's television screens. A simple logical review of events that led to the attack shows how neatly the incident had been planned from within the highest offices of the US and other foreign Governments, and not by a bogus boogeyman from a cave in Afghanistan using cell phones and walkie-talkies to coordinate such an event.

This is an example of the power of thought launched into the mass consciousness. When such a thought-form carries the truth and is well-enough formulated with enough correct details, it attracts the mental matter necessary to make it grow. The analysis done by the engineers and architects is an example of how the thought-form gathered supporting mental matter to complete itself. A more and more complete rendition of the 9/11 incident has now been formulated from the seeds that were planted a decade ago and is now being broadcasted around the world to receptive minds via the mass consciousness.

The Power of Thought to Effect Change

At this point in our journey toward the New Age, many of us feel powerless against the overwhelming structure of physical and mental control the Dark Forces have at their disposal. But if there is anything in the world that is more powerful than the whole Dark Force arsenal, it is still the power of thought. This is the weapon that everyone is equipped to use during the ongoing battle with the forces of darkness. It is even more powerful than street riots or demonstrations against human injustices, although such demonstrations serve as landmarks to measure the state of change in the ongoing transmutation of matter. Thought is also the creative tool that can be used to manifest all one needs.

The key to the thought-form's power is its clarity and detail. The Master, who once taught in London and Boston as depicted in the *Initiate* series by Cyril Scott and known to us under his earthly pseudonym as Justin Moreward Haig, gave the author the simple formula for using thought-forms:

> . . . (W)e, who worship at the feet of great Buddhas, find them contemplating this simple truth. You see, there is something of a mystery here. That which passes for the simple is often the most profound. When I say then that all things begin with thought, I speak of creation from beginning to end. The clothes that you are wearing were once a thought in a designer's mind. Now they adorn your form. . . . There is much that I would say to you about thought, but it lies here. But whatever you want to accomplish, first think of it specifically as only a thought. You see in this there is confusion. First, it must be seen as the thought form that it is and only then, once the thought is clear can atoms know how to proceed to build molecules of matter around the thought-form. So you see the thought itself must be intact, clear, and as definite as one can make it. [22]

The power of thought is very much underestimated and the tendency among lightbearers is to think that we are individually too insignificant to make a difference. But with an understanding of cycles and cosmic trends given to us in the Ancient Wisdom, our thinking can be

---

[22] A private interview with the author.

put in harmony with what we know of the Divine Plan, and within that plan, we can generate thought-forms of quality and detail that can turn the battle with the Dark Forces in favour of the forces of light.

Creating thought-forms to manifest one's needs is also a valid right, but this creative process has been twisted into yet another New Age industry that commercializes spiritual teachings. Through high-powered and expensive seminars, marketing experts prey on well-intentioned lightbearers to use "the secret" of the Law of Attraction to satisfy one's selfish desires and become part of the super wealthy. Creating thought-forms to manifest a gated mansion with a swimming pool and two sports cars parked in the driveway is quite different from creating thought-forms that will shed light on the lies and projects that the Dark Forces perpetrate against one's brethren.

Seeding the Mass Consciousness

The mass consciousness exists on the lower mental plane and often works in tandem with the astral plane. Lower astral emotions permeate the lower mental plane, oscillating between mental and astral matter. The mass consciousness thus mirrors the fact that the vast majority of the earth's populations live according to emotional impulses and basic mental functions necessary to survive which provides ready fodder to the Dark Forces.

Invocation of Light into the Mass Consciousness

As world karma plays out, we, the inhabitants of the earth, have the right to invoke light and help from the Spiritual Hierarchy. We have the right to think the truth about what is going on, no matter what the mass media is telling us. Finally, we have the right and power to send our enlightened thoughts into the mass consciousness, without hatred or emotion but as a matter of duty, being lightbearers in incarnation on earth. This whole thought process is done internally far from the eyes of the Dark Forces and has the incalculable force of the cosmos behind it.

Once we release these light-bearing thoughts into the mass consciousness, they find their way into the open-minded of similar vibrations. This is the true working of the Law of Attraction. Through this marvellous cosmic law, the light-bearing thought-form works its way through the often dark recesses of mass consciousness and begins to reach more and more lightbearers and the open-minded around the world. The momentum builds and a snowball effect ensues.

Each enlightened thought-form works to counter the lies and deception that are resident in the mass consciousness, AND IT IS IN THE MASS CONSCIOUSNESS THAT THE INITIAL HEALING OF THE EARTH'S MENTAL BODY TAKES PLACE.

The mass consciousness can reach more individuals than the mass media and can gain considerable momentum in shifting the balance of light and darkness on earth. It will touch the minds of people in their sleep, in quiet moments of contemplation during the day, in prayers, and even in the most unexpected moments of one's daily life. And as minds change, so will the rebalancing begin to manifest on the earth plane.

The Dark Forces know of this power and fight process by creating every conceivable form of noise and real and virtual distractions to create confusion. They even direct their agents on the astral plane to whisper counter-thoughts that seem like one's own thinking. Thus, they, too, feed the mass consciousness with lies, half-truths and sophisms. To make these distractions stick, they project anything that titillates the lower chakras so that thinking is held in sensual chains.

But those who see beyond these counter-claims can form the initial snowball whose momentum and size will eventually overwhelm these Dark Forces efforts. The mass consciousness will reform and thus represent the true thoughts of earth's inhabitants.

What you can do . . .

Below is the Invocation against the Dark Forces, a gift from the Spiritual Hierarchy. This invocation strikes at every activity the Dark Forces are engaged in and provides the divine solutions to them. You can use each stanza or groups of stanzas to build more substantial thought-forms based on your own experience and understanding.

Here is what you can do:

1. Study the invocation stanza by stanza
2. Focus on one or two stanzas per day: understand it and meditate on it. Add to it from your observation of the news and experience.
3. Once you understand the stanza in sufficient detail, launch your thought-form into the mass consciousness.
4. Launching the thought-form: Imagine the thought-form is like a balloon that is rising up to the mass consciousness. Once there, it explodes and sends its thought-forms rippling through the mass consciousness.

There are enough stanzas to keep you busy for a full month. Once you terminate the whole invocation, return to the beginning and do as many months of invocation that you deem necessary as part of your effort to seed the mass consciousness.

The thought-forms that each of us sends up to the mass consciousness will, through the Law of Attraction, find those of similar vibrations around the world who are willing to entertain them, adopt them and take action. It will reach lightbearers who have been placed on the front lines of activities financed and promoted by the Dark Forces.

As these thought-forms fill with the understanding and power you give them and spread, the mass consciousness, for all its good and evil, becomes transformed, but even before this great transformation, it does its job of "distributing" the thought-forms that you have sent up to those of like vibrations.

Invocation Against the Dark Forces

Oh, living light of love,
Oh, great and Holy Divine Mother
That IS the sweetness of life itself,
Come, come, come
Into the Earth plane as never before.

Come, O dear Cosmic Mother!
Enfold us all.
Take us all into your wondrous embrace.
Comfort us and give us the strength
And the bravery to be who we truly are -
Beings of Love, Forgiveness, Joy, and Laughter.
And, O Divine Mother,
Bring your broom and sweep clean the earth
Of all those who do not respect thee,
Of all those misguided children,
For they are your children as well,
Who have foolishly taken the Dark Path
Of domination, oppression, and the
Unbalanced manifestations of masculine energy.

Let the Feminine Ray arise!
Let the Feminine Ray be glorified.
Let the Feminine Ray come into ultimate power.
And may there be, now,
A very powerful Karmic readjustment on this planet,
On earth as it is in Heaven.

That all those who want to dominate others
Who want to oppress others,
Who want to punish others,

Who tend towards cruelty, malice, torture,
And all forms of such evil-doing,
Let these know the just judgment
Of the Lord God and his Minions of Light.

Let the Great Archangel Michael
Now swoop onto the earth
Bringing his numberless legions of angels
And wipe clean the earth
Of those who will not stop in their fighting
In their terrorism of others
And in their lies toward their brethren.

Let all the layers of Darkness be exposed
To the fullest light of truth.
And let all world leaders who are inclined to war,
Who are inclined to collaborate with those dark forces
That up to this point have controlled
The money and the power on this planet,
Let these be given a choice.

Dispatch Angels to them as they sleep,
Bright messengers that will awaken them
And say to them "You, who head the country,
Be AWARE.

The CHOICE is upon you now:
Shall you continue to be in the camp of these Dark Ones,
That would war and take and lie and kill?
For if so, you shall go down with them as well,
And quickly at that!

If you have the heart,
If you have the mind,

To see that this is not
The way of Light, Love, and Joy
And have the bravery to change your stance,
Do something of true worth for your country,
Then you will be a leader, indeed.

Otherwise, prepare to lose all that you have.
And that will, in all likelihood,
Include your physical life as well.
For there can be no further toleration
Of that Evil which delights in malice.

Now let the avalanche of Karma
Be released upon all those
Who will not even for the moment
Consider changing their hard-hearted
And hard-headed attitudes.

And may these be returned to the Spirit Realm
For they can be educated and re-programmed
For such things do not work,
Never have worked
And never shall work.

O Divine Mother, come personally.
Touch our hearts.
Enlighten us all that we might see
That TOLERANCE is beautiful.
But it does no good
When it is expended upon those
Who have no tolerance for anyone but themselves.

Let now the Lords of Karma
Move mightily and swiftly

And stop these who would
Perpetrate only further warfare
And manipulations of this population.

We call for the All Seeing Eye of God
To expose them on the media,
In front of everyone;
We call for the All Seeing Eye of God
To expose the sham that they are behind.

The facade that they have created
And all of that which occurred
Upon the 11th of September
Of the Year 2001
Which was not what it was portrayed to be.

Let there be an exposure now
From the very depths.
Let them ALL be shown
For precisely who and what they are --
Perpetrators of lies.

Those who are the reincarnated
Sons of Belial of Atlantis
And those who have come here from other planets
And have simply been handed the reins
By the so-called leaders of the countries of the earth plane.
Let there now be a sorting and a sifting,
Guided and directed by
The Great and Holy Master Jesus himself.

Let him bring his mighty sword and sever ties,
If necessary, familial ties,
That keep the truly sweet, forgiving, and innocent bound

To those who are inclined and prone to
Dominate, harm, lie, cheat, steal, oppress,
And do all those things
Which have nothing to do with the Christ.

And may the Great Lord Buddha,
Lord of the World also be ensconced in full glory,
Radiating his Golden Light of Wisdom
So that ALL rise and see clearly
How they have been lied to.

How they have been foolish
In trusting such as these!
How they need to have questioned
Authority wherever they found it!
And only when they could hear
Truth ringing in their own hearts
Would they have been justified
In being satisfied with such as these.

Let God's will be done in all matters,
And let the Judgment be swift,
Specifically upon all those who align themselves
With institutions such as the IRS
Which unjustly take monies
From those who need it most.

Let their charge now be this:
That we, the People of Earth,
NOW do charge institutions such as the IRS
With stealing food out of the mouths of children who need
it,
With stealing food from the elderly

And those who cannot work,
And using it to create war and war-like machines.

We DEMAND that they be
Brought to account this very hour,
That they all be held accountable
For every drop of blood
For which they are responsible
And for every war they have ever instigated
Simply to generate money.

Let the Living God Almighty
Within each one of us RISE up as never before.
And be UNITED as a wall of fire
That burns, burns, burns
Right through their façade,
Right through their compounds,
Melting their computers,
Causing them, each one, to go running in fear.

For At Last,
The Lord of Righteousness
Is upon the doorstep
And demanding explanation
For their evil deeds and actions.

We will not tolerate it for one more second.
We demand Justice now.
Let them be the ones who are on the run and not we.
Let them be the ones who are now scattering,
Running to so many peaks,
Hiding from the ones
Who would bring them to their just end.

Let these things occur,
Now and forever more
Until the planet is as it was always meant to be:
A Garden of Beauty, a place of Love, Joy,
That terra might join her sisters and brothers
In the cosmic parade of planets liberated.

And may the Great and Holy Master Saint Germain,
The Lord of Freedom for the Earth,
Hurl his mighty Miracle Pouch into the governments
Of every single country that currently exists.
And consume with the Violet Flame all of that which is
unrighteous,
Its causes, its cores, its seeds, its effects
And all its memories connected therewith.

Let God's will be done.
Let the Light of Freedom alone guide
This wondrous parade of light.
And may the Lords of Karma answer our call.
And once and for all bring us back to Love, Love, Love,
and Love
So be it forever more.   Amen

* * *

Formulating your own Thought-forms of Truth against Corruption

Seeding the mass consciousness with correct thought-forms concerning your home region can also lead to very specific and local effects. As lightbearers you represent the truth. Your innate sense of what is right and wrong stems from soul experience that dates back millennia. Any sign of corruption, no matter how petty, bothers you, and if it comes into your experience, you are being given the opportunity to correct it. Others would shrug it off as "the way things are," but you cannot take it that lightly.

Corruption permeates all levels of our society today. This is because our top leaders are corrupt and immoral, and this lack of morality filters down through society and tempts all who have some modicum of power.

The mayor of your town is suspected of fraud or embezzlement. A respected member of the community, an investment advisor, bilks his customers of millions. Others promote investment schemes of every sort blandly stealing billions from their customers. These are the examples of corruption that hit the newspapers. However, other acts either go unnoticed or are deemed too petty to make a fuss about. The town or county official may be submitting reimbursement claims that exaggerate actual expenditures. The clerk in charge of lost and found objects may be taking the found objects for his or her personal use. The staff at the local thrift shop store might be keeping all the valuable donations for itself and putting the junk up for sale to the public. The vegetable vendor might fix his scale ever so slightly to cheat his customers of a few cents on market day. New age gurus, pundits, psychics and mediums charge important sums for spurious information that was given to them by unprincipled astral entities. The list goes on and on, and unless these seemingly innocuous cases of corruption are wiped out on all levels of the society, the earth cannot move on.

Everyone, especially lightbearers, must become aware of both the greater and lesser presence of corruption and not be afraid to speak the truth, especially in small towns and rural communities where "rocking the boat" might upset friends and neighbours with hidden vested interests. The lightbearer need not get into a fight with the people involved but can be aware of the details that are transpiring.

With no constraints, the lightbearer can meditate upon these cases of corruption and send the corrected idea up to the mass consciousness. How many similar cases of corruption can that corrected idea reach around the world? Millions, including the specific case you are involved with. The truth can be surprisingly specific and general at the same time!

Warriors of a Different Ilk

Lightbearers who make up the ranks of the Master St. Germain's Forces of Light wield the same "weapons" as the great Buddhas of our era: thought-forms laden with truth. The battleground on the earth plane takes place first in the mass consciousness which, unfortunately, the Dark Forces have dominated for too long. Any evil action played out on the earth plane originates from an evil thought and conversely any good and truthful action originates from a good and truthful thought. An evil thought-form can be neutralized by its counterpart truth thought-form, and the victory is assured.

An evil and heavily armed military force can be undermined if the thought-forms that have created it are neutralized or destroyed by thought-forms of the light bearing knowledge of such weapons. So a light-bearing thought-form must be carefully thought out or plotted in detail to assure its effectiveness.

Much implied here is that the lightbearer must be informed yet not emotionally involved with the information he or she is creating in the thought-form. The lightbearer's creation must be based on cosmic law, be in line with his or her knowledge of the Divine Plan and be laden with the material knowledge of the case in point. If the thought-form involves economics, then the information about economics must be sound and truthful. If the government is colluding with the Dark Forces banking sector and stealing billions of the people's money, then the lightbearer or groups of lightbearers must formulate informed thought-forms of good governance and banking to counter these actions. This is the kind of active thought-warrior that is demanded of the forces of light. Like David before Goliath, anyone who wishes to take on the task of bringing down the banking sector can do so by seeding the mass consciousness with all the good thought-forms that counter this specific type of collusion. But the creators of these principle-laden thought-forms must be rightly informed in all aspects, esoterically and non-esoterically, of the specific matter at hand. Again we reiterate what the Master JMH said on this matter:

> . . . First, it must be seen as the thought form that it is and only then, once the thought is clear can atoms know how to proceed to build molecules of

matter around the thought-form. So you see the thought itself must be intact, clear, and as definite as one can make it. I speak of these things, for I find that the few stumbling blocks that you tend to encounter will tend to come because that which has been attempted has not been clearly thought out. Not as clearly as it might. Let all things then be seen for what they are---thoughts, thoughts, thoughts . . .[23]

Thought Missiles

The building of complex thought-forms can come as a result of a book written on a particular subject, a website blog, a letter written to the authorities about a certain observed crime, an observation, a private research project and a reaction to the news. Once thought out in detail, the thought-form, to be ever effective, must be consciously sent to the mass consciousness like a "thought missile."

Both evil and good thought-forms exist in earth's duality, but the good thought-forms are endowed with the upper hand in any battle that involves the two. We must expect the evil thought-form to resist and not go down without a struggle. Riding out its noise and clatter might be difficult and this is when most give up. Evil appears to take over only when the good thought-form gives up too soon or remains dormant due to negligence, apathy or acquiescence.

---

[23] Ibid.

Persistence in formulating the thought-form is itself a challenge. Actively seeding the mass consciousness with well-conceived, detailed thought-forms is probably the most powerful weapon against evil that exists. Undermine the evil action by undermining the very thought-form that supports it, and you have won the battle. The defeat is manifested on the earth plane.

Lightbearers cannot expect to win a popularity contest, either. In fact, they are likely to be swimming against the tide in most cases. At all times, they must use wisdom in voicing their thoughts. Most of the time, adopting silence might be the best way to act when among friends and family. However, in the silence of your meditation space, you can create powerful, well-constructed thought-forms that can have a major impact on the events of the world and in your community.

In sum, as warriors of a different ilk, lightbearers can actively observe, meditate, teach and speak out in the name of principle, and in doing so, they create the seeds of thought-forms that can be sent like thought missiles into the mass consciousness and from thereon be distributed worldwide.

Invoking the Aid of the Spiritual Hierarchy

The Masters of Wisdom stand ready to help the lightbearer only if the lightbearer takes the first steps to gather and think through information needed for the thought-form formulation. This includes investing time and effort acquiring a working knowledge of the Ancient Wisdom, for it is a combination of earthly and spiritual knowledge anchored in the ages that will undermine the workings of the Dark Forces.

By respect and adherence to the Cosmic Law of Free Will, the Spiritual Hierarchy must remain outside any specific battle that you are involved in, *until you invoke their help.* When invoked, they will put at lightbearers' disposal all the resources they need to formulate the thought-form or prevail in the battle. They are given access to information as well as reminded of certain cosmic laws and principles involved. So it is important to remember to invoke the aid of the Spiritual Hierarchy if needed.

Aiding the Transmutation of Concrete Matter

The transmutation of concrete matter is change, and seeding the mass consciousness with principle-laden thought-forms in our battle against the Dark Forces helps bring about the transformation of the earth we so desire. This is not an overnight affair, for even after the battle with the Dark Forces has been won, the continued effort of the lightbearers to seed the mass consciousness from the Spiritual Regions will be necessary to bring the world into balance. Will this balance be achieved by 2050-2060? It will all depend on how we shape the mass consciousness by that time.

Chapter 6

Navigating Through Turmoil

We now have an idea of where civilisation is heading in the Divine Plan and what we can do to determine the direction of this journey as the financial and economic systems collapse and the world anticipates war and earth changes. All have a part in transmuting dense matter of the third dimension into lighter matter on the way to the fourth dimension.

During the next fifty years, we must expect more "rockin' and rollin'" and society will continue to experience waves of emotions that will whipsaw the individual and knock him or her off kilter daily. You, as a lightbearer in the midst of this chaos, must develop your inner fortitude not only to pull through this period intact, but also to exercise the leadership that you contracted to provide during this period. Essentially, you must master bringing into your conscious thinking your divine plan.

The magnitude of the changes ahead of us is such that we can no longer depend on governments, bureaucracies, charitable organizations and the like for help. These organizations, including private ones, will all break down. The only sustainable leadership in this transition will come from lightbearers who are firmly in touch with their souls and who can keep centered and inwardly peaceful while surrounded by chaos.

The path leading to a conscious realization of your mission on earth during these times will be fraught with obstacles. As we mentioned in Volume 2, your incarnation has already been targeted, and a bevy of distractions and obstacles has been strewn before you in order to veer you off the path. This is a fact in many of your lives. Many of you have been debilitated by entity possession, dysfunctional relationships and marriages, long-standing money problems that have been exacerbated by the economic crisis and/or just plain old laziness. Nobody "promised you a rose garden" when you volunteered to reincarnate during this period and you still have a choice, after all, to either fulfill your mission or pass back out of incarnation with the onerous reputation of "Mission UN-accomplished".

We have stressed the need to anchor yourself in the Ancient Wisdom, not as another form of religious indoctrination, but as a way to develop your consciousness and mind so that it can better discern lies from the truth, sophism from wisdom and distraction and deception from the true path. Pseudo-spiritual teachings designed to empty your pocketbook are rampant, but if not based solidly on cosmic law will eventually fall by the wayside. In the meantime you have wasted valuable time and effort being waylaid temporarily off the path. Most lightbearers will eventually return to their path and mission, even after being temporarily distracted by a myriad of strategies the Dark Forces promote.

Honouring Amon Ra and Your Soul

Of paramount importance today is for all of us to re-establish contact with the Sun God of our solar system, Amon Ra, for the "God Within" or "I AM" of which we constantly speak emanates from Him.   Of equal importance is His feminine counterpart, Vesta.   Together they represent the perfect balance between feminine and masculine characteristics that rule our solar system and which earth, deep down, emulates.

The ultimate creator of the Universe, who is often referred to in the Ancient Wisdom as Brahma is too great for our puny minds to conceive of.[24]   So great is the universe of His creation that we are told there are fifteen trillion (15,000,000,000,000) solar systems each with a central sun, great soul like our Sun God, Amon Ra!

So, during the ups and downs of our lives here on planet earth we rejoice that we have so direct a representative God such as Amon Ra, so much so that every morning we awaken to see and feel the great warmth of the Sun that represents the presence of His physical manifested body.

---

[24] There are some today who claim to be in direct contact with the Great Brahma.   These unfortunate ones suffer from great delusions borne primarily of their own egos. Such a direct communication would immediately annihilate the claimant as the power of Brahma is like no other.

During most of the first half of the Fourth Round, most ancient civilisations worshipped the Sun God as a given. Testaments to their worship can be found all around the world, in temples, pyramids, and icons. Gradually the worship of the great Sun God was ridiculed out of existence in favour of other conjured up images emanating from human religions to justify the connections their clergy had with God.

Modern civilisation, especially the Fifth Root-Race has seen fit to replace the Sun with science and rational thinking despite the daily sunrises and sunsets that are so obvious to our senses. Even the most elementary science necessarily concludes that without the Sun, there would be no life on earth. So this fundamental recognition of Amon Ra as the very source of life itself to all on earth must return to the general consciousness of mankind as a pre-condition to entering the New Age.

The Origin of the "God Within"

The truth, "We are the sons and daughters of God" must again be honoured in the New Age. The Sun, Amon Ra, emits billions of rays, each ray carries the entire characteristics and substance of the Sun, just as a drop of sea water carries all the properties of the ocean. This ray or spark of the Sun is called a monad and each ray streams across the vast space of the solar system and lodges in each and every one of us as the lifeline that connects us directly to Amon Ra and to life itself.

In the physical world, all depend on the physical Sun, for without it all life would cease on earth. This is the outer analogy that belies the inner world's organisation. In the inner world, each monad passes through the finest and most spiritual parts of our beings and makes its way down through our mental, astral, etheric and finally physical bodies. On the way down, this unique ray or monad incarnates as the soul in the high mental-spiritual-buddhic matter of our bodies.

> . . . from the "mineral" monad up to the time when that monad blossoms forth by evolution into the DIVINE MONAD . . . it is still one and the same Monad, differing only in its incarnations, throughout its ever succeeding cycles of partial or total obscuration of spirit, or the partial or total obscuration of matter—two polar antitheses—as it ascends into the realms of mental spirituality, or descends into the depths of materiality."[25]

The soul then stretches its energies into the dense vibrations of matter that form the etheric and physical bodies. Finally, in the physical body, the soul establishes a foothold in the pineal gland in the centre of the brain.[26] From the pineal gland, the soul maintains the connection between the physical body and the monad and reigns as the "God Within". Thus the connection from the pineal gland in the brain all the way to the Amon Ra, the Sun, remains intact, eternal and inviolable, a miracle in and of itself.

---

[25] Blavatsky, H.P. *op. cit.*, v. 1, p. 175

[26] Many New Age pundits wrongly place the soul's foothold in the heart.

We can say then, that the soul is the first incarnation of the monad and is individualized in high vibrational matter that is invisible to the physical body's senses, yet it sends down impulses to the physical body's subconscious and conscious minds. These impulses manifest physically in the form of knowledge, thought-forms and intuition.

This is what the Master Jesus meant when he declared, "Ye are the temple of God." Our physical bodies encase something wondrous: "the God Within" in the pineal gland of your brain, your private prelate in your sacred private temple.

The Goal of the Next Fifty Years

The goal of the next fifty years is for mankind to achieve conscious contact with the soul that will allow its expression through our physical vehicles. This expression will necessarily translate into your individual plan and mission.

The impulses or intuitions you receive from the soul are rational and enlightening, not emotionally induced. Receiving a soul impulse is like a light bulb going off in your head, and the knowledge it conveys to you is something you just know. This minute but sustaining instance of enlightenment is what gives you that moment of supreme satisfaction and feeling of high love. It is sweet and wonderful, but not emotional.

Be not fooled by frauds and charlatan psychics or even well-meaning mediums who claim to read your soul purpose. If you cannot communicate with your own soul, how can these strangers? It's just logical. What is required is that you make a conscious decision to take the journey into your inner world through meditation and find out for yourself what this individualized part of the great Sun God, Amon Ra, knows of your individual divine plan.

It would stand to reason that if you were to establish contact with your soul and allow it to express itself through your physical personality, you would have the God of our solar system on your side throughout the upheaval and turmoil of the transition into the New Age. What more could you ask for and what more could you want?

Control Your Mind--The First Step

For many decades the Dark Forces have perfected techniques of mind control and manipulation. The post-World War II communist regimes experimented and used mind-bending techniques that included mass propaganda through all known means of media communication, mind manipulation and control, peer pressure and torture, mind bending indoctrination, drugs, and the omniscient public loudspeakers that indoctrinated the people from the minute they woke up until they could escape into their dreams. The final nail in the coffin of this control was to ration how much food a person could eat through food ration tickets and to determine their jobs.

Today, as the Dark Forces are cornered, it is not surprising to see more sophisticated mind-bending techniques being used in the so-called democratic "free" world.

The mass media does not tell the truth but taints facts to spin whatever they want the readers to believe in accordance with the vast governmental collusion with the Dark Forces. They know how to manipulate the most vulnerable part of our bodies today, the astral or emotional body, and propaganda techniques are aimed at the emotional/astral body to create fear and trembling, horror, sexual obsessions, cravings, loathing, racism, and even false hopes---whatever works to keep people off keel, dumb and disunited in human society. This is what we must cope with today.

The Internet, that great invention of the Master St. Germain, has provided an excellent means to break the hegemony of the mass media; however the Dark Forces are also ramping up their efforts to take over this information source. As more and more newspapers and other traditional forms of media crumble in the global financial crisis, these media are resorting to the Internet as their main distribution channel. So there is a growing danger of too much information being centralized on the Internet which could become yet another tool of mind manipulation. Of all the millions of stories a newspaper could print daily, we notice that the major newspapers of the world seem to report the same news as one another. Recent events have demonstrated how countries can control information passing through the Internet and it is evident that the Dark Force monopoly of computer operating systems enables them to gain control of this tool of freedom.

Keeping up with events is a challenge because of this monopoly on information. But even propaganda needs some facts upon which to build a story. And with other new technologies of individual communications, it is very difficult to hide obvious events such as food riots, tax revolts, coups d'état, revolutions, etc. Nevertheless, even the choice of facts and how the media use them to construct a news story can be used to slant the news, create false impressions, and play on the emotions so that it steers your thinking in a certain way. The lightbearer must filter through this maze of information and discern what is truth and what are lies.

Things will get worse before the final axe comes down on the Dark Forces, and mankind is free from their regime. Lightbearers cannot succumb to these tactics but must learn to navigate their way through this turmoil in order to survive intact. If not, they cannot do what they came here to do and that is to reconstruct the society for the New Age.

Navigating our way through this tough period of turmoil will be a challenge, but there are some surprisingly simple ways the Ancient Wisdom provides us so that we can wend our way through mind manipulation and maintain our god-given free will and independence. As we said above, with the God of our Solar System, Amon Ra, on our side, what more could we ask for?

Shielding Yourself from Mass Emotional Manipulation

A famous pop star or political figure suddenly dies and mass funeral rites are televised worldwide. Media stars shed tears on stage and sing to a world audience that is sucked into a vortex of sadness, loss, regret, and nostalgia while the orchestra plays tunes that tug at your heartstrings. TV audiences in the farthest corners of the earth convulse into tears in their living rooms. In another instance, the final rounds of the World Cup games annually grips the world, conveying conflict, high combative emotions, hatred, division, separateness, resulting in some cases in looting, vandalism and even death. In another instance, a famous Indian guru makes an appearance in a huge public park, his wife bedecked with gold jewellery sits next to him on a gilded stage. Like sheep, hordes encircle the stage around him chanting and marching and preying upon his every precious word. Tears of devotion flow from their eyes as their emotions take control and they succumb to the guru's words . . . and they willingly open their pocketbooks in gratitude. All these examples provide fodder for astral plane entities to feast on and more opportunities for mind manipulation as emotions override clear thinking.

The mass media brings into each home mass emotional event through television. We should be suspicious of any such events, for they require the enormous sums of financial backing and organisation that only the Dark Forces have today. The only way to draw huge worldwide audiences is to prey on the emotional body through astral manipulation of the "emotional hook". Looking more deeply, we see that the real purpose of these events is to anchor mankind more to the dense material world through the person's astral or emotional body.

The rule of thumb for a lightbearer is to head in the opposite direction of mass events and gatherings. While the crowds rush in one direction, the lightbearer should move in the opposite direction or simply turn off the television or computer dishing the event to you. Mass emotions have no *raison d'être* except to manipulate mankind for more insidious purposes. If you feel drawn in the same direction as the masses, then you are succumbing to mind manipulation. This rule applies not only to mass gatherings but also to mass fashion trends, the latest rage or the latest popular flavour of the month.

Throughout this long tumultuous period, the lightbearers must develop and maintain independence of thinking and the ability to go against the popular wave while the rest of the world is in a panic. It is for that reason that the control of the mind is of paramount importance.

Taking Control of your Mind

Information coming into your life through television, radio, background noises and the internet is relatively easy to switch off, provided you do not have a psychological dependence on them. Regaining control of your mind from the myriad of distractions around you gives you the rudder that will help you navigate through the sea of chaos in the coming years.

Developing the Ability to Concentrate

Like the stabilizers on a ship navigating through a tempest, the ability to concentrate is the step to regain control over you mind and the key to surviving the turmoil that is ahead. As acceleration continues to burrow into each nook and cranny of life, upheavals will continue to strike at all levels of society. Not one person will escape the changes wrought by acceleration.

As life unfolds daily there are countless distractions that grab at your conscious mind making it flit from distraction to distraction. Tasks and duties get waylaid and remain unfinished. You become forgetful. Perhaps you walk all the way downstairs for a reason and cannot remember what you went there for. You set out to do something and minutes later you end up involved in something else. You dart from project to project never really finishing any of them.

These distractions are often astrally induced as your astral or emotional body whipsaws with the general waves flashing through the astral plane. When it comes to lightbearers, who are often targets of the Dark Forces, these distractions become more deliberate attempts to veer you off course for the day or even for the rest of your life. Those who are psychically inclined, as are a lot of lightbearers, are especially prone to this type of astral manipulation. So the ability to rein in the ever-flitting conscious mind is in great need today in order to counter mental confusion and unfocused activity during your waking hours. Moreover, an easily distracted mind often leads to graver problems such as depression, addiction, and a host of psychosomatic diseases.

Below we recommend three simple ways you might adopt to help you build up your ability to concentrate.

1. The Seven Inhalations and Exhalations

We recommend a very useful exercise that neophyte Tibetan Buddhists use to rein in the conscious mind. This technique is useful to regain your ability to concentrate, a first step in controlling your conscious mind. It consists simply of breathing in and out seven times without losing your concentration. As you master this technique, you will bring your conscious mind under YOUR control and from there, you will be able to benefit from deeper forms of meditation.

1. Find a quiet spot in your home where you can go to without being interrupted.
2. Sit quietly for a couple minutes and take a couple deep breaths to calm down your body
3. Tell yourself that you are now going to take seven deep inhalations and exhalations without letting your mind wander.
4. Concentrate solely on your breathing in and out, nothing else.
5. Take deep breath number one. Exhale. Concentrate on that breath and its exhalation.
6. Take deep breath number two and exhale. Chances are your mind has already flitted to

another subject. If not, go on to the third, then fourth and up to the seventh.

7. Whenever your mind flits during this exercise, stop and return to inhalation number one and start all over again! You may be startled to discover that your mind begins to flit even after the first breath. Getting pass the third breath without the mind flitting is already an accomplishment and you're almost halfway there!

Be honest with yourself when you realize that your mind has broken concentration and go back to the first breath. Rein it in like you would a wild horse and try to finish the seven inhalations and exhalations without losing a mini-second of your concentration.

In the beginning, you will be surprised how independent and wild your conscious mind is from your desired control. This should indicate to you that your mind needs to come under YOUR control rather than be subject to the multiple distractions in your life and thus subject to Dark Forces manipulation. But don't feel burdened by the mind's seeming uncooperative activity in the beginning. Keep a light attitude and do not be discouraged early on because your efforts will surely bear fruit if you persist, and you'll reach the end of the seventh breath with full control.

Do this exercise at least once a day, more if possible. Do it while you're waiting for someone or when you have a pause in your daily life, even when you are stuck in traffic or waiting at a dentist's office.

As you gain more and more control over your mind, you should begin to entertain positive changes in your life and know how to deal with family or business crises as they arise. Moreover, you will know that you have taken a major step to gaining dominion over your conscious mind and your life on earth.

2. Seed Thought Meditation

After you have successfully conquered the seven inhalations and exhalations and you have a better control on your conscious mind, you can move on to a seed thought meditation.

1. Pick a thought on which you would like to meditate, e.g. your divine service, your mission in life, money, a business challenge, a relationship problem or any thought that seems to preoccupy you at the moment. Pick only one thought to meditate on. If you feel emotional about the seed thought, try to calm down the emotions as best you can.

2. Sit in your quiet spot and complete the seven inhalations and exhalations as preparation for your seed-thought meditation. By this time your conscious mind should be reined in for this meditation.

3. Now, focus on this seed idea, bringing all your concentration upon it. You may need to visualize the word that represents the thought, i.e. "mission" or "money". Do not allow your

emotions to cloud the issue, just focus on the thought.

4. As you concentrate on the word or idea, you can break it down and analyze it or you can just concentrate on it until it breaks down itself and you see it more profoundly. You are now getting into the essence of the thought-form behind the problem.

5. Probe deeper into the thought-form with the same focus and concentration.

6. As you probe deeper, the thought should yield its own solution or manifest a resolution in your life. Many of life's problems can be resolved in this manner, especially those which seem intractable during this tumultuous period.

3. Practice Yoga

The art and science of yoga must have been invented for these tumultuous days, for it remains one of the best aids to gaining control of your mind and body after so many centuries. Many men in the West, for some strange reason, think that yoga practice is a "girl thing". Could it be that they simply do not want to lose face when they discover how stiff and rigid their physical bodies are? If men shun the practice of yoga for whatever reason, they are losing out on one of the most beneficial sciences of mind control that is available.

Which Yoga system should you practice? In most yoga studios in the West, the practice has come to mean a kind of physical callisthenics with lip service paid to a quick meditation after a set of sweaty exercises or *asanas*. Variations of the physical aspect of yoga have even taken on an almost masochistic practice such as pumping up the room temperature to make you sweat profusely while doing the poses.

In reality the *asanas* are just a part of the whole meaning of yoga, which is UNION, and are practiced in combination with diet, meditation and mental discipline to aid the seeker to unify all the bodies that are operating on the earth plane —physical, etheric, astral, mental and spiritual. If achieved, such a union enables the soul to shine through and express itself through all the bodies, especially through the physical. This is no better explained than in Patanjali's sacred sutras on Raja Yoga, the King of Yogas, the preferred and recommended form of yoga for this age, because it contains all the previous systems of Yogas.

Here is what the Master Djwal Khul said of the various yoga practices:

All the various Yogas have had their place in the unfoldment of the human being. In the first purely physical race, which is called the Lemurian, the Yoga at that time imposed upon infant humanity was Hatha Yoga, the Yoga of the physical body, that Yoga which brings into conscious use and manipulation the various organs, muscles and parts of the physical frame. The problem before the adepts of that time was to teach human beings, who were then little more than animals, the purpose, significance and use of their various organs, so that they could consciously control

167

them, and the meaning of the symbol of the human figure. Therefore, in those early days, through the practice of Hatha Yoga, the human being reached the portal of initiation. At that time the attainment of the third initiation, resulting in the transfiguration of the personality, was the highest initiation that man was capable of achieving.

In the Atlantean days, the progress of the sons of men was procured through the imposition of two Yogas. First, the Yoga which is called by the name of Laya Yoga, the Yoga of the centres which produced a stabilizing of the etheric body and of the centres in man and the development of the astral and psychic nature. Later on, Bhakti Yoga, growing out of the development of the emotional or astral body, was incorporated with Laya Yoga and the foundation of that mysticism and devotion, which has been the underlying incentive during our particular Aryan root race, was laid. The fourth initiation was at that time the objective. The subject of these initiations has been discussed more at length in my previous volume, "Initiation, Human and Solar".

Now, in the Aryan race, the subjugation of the mental body and the control of the mind are brought about through the practice of Raja Yoga, and the fifth initiation, that of adept, is the goal for evolving humanity. Thus, all the Yogas have had their place and served a useful purpose and it will become apparent that any return to Hatha Yoga practices or those practices which deal specifically with the development of the centers, brought about through various types of meditation practices and breathing exercises is, from a certain aspect, retrogression. It will be found that through the practice of Raja Yoga, and through assuming that point of directional control which is to be found by the man who centers his consciousness in the soul, the other forms of Yoga are unnecessary, for the greater Yoga automatically includes all the lesser in its results, though not in its practices.[27]

Highly recommended reading is *The Art and Science of Raja Yoga* by Swami Kriyananda (J. Donald Walters) based in the teachings of Paramhansa Yogananda.

Handling Entity Possession

Your astral or emotional body responds to the overall astral plane of the earth and as acceleration ramps up and passes through the astral plane, it roils and agitates the astral plane as well as your emotional body. Mind is the primary way to control your astral body. If you cannot control your conscious mind, your astral or emotional body will swing with the agitation on the astral plane and you will feel up and down as waves of agitation sweep through the astral plane. Without knowing why your moods change from hour to hour, day to day, you may feel that you have lost control of yourself. Such is life under the regime of the emotional body.

---

[27] Alice A. Bailey, *The Light of the Soul, The Yoga Sutras of Patanjali,* New York: Lucis Publishing Co.,1997, pp, x-xi.

Soulless astral shells and entities that inhabit the astral plane are very much at risk of being wiped out by acceleration. They are scrambling to survive, and their alternative source of energy to keep themselves from deteriorating may be YOU. They will latch onto people in order to draw in pranic energy from the person's etheric body. They can take over your body and cause obsessive and insane behaviour; addiction to alcohol, drugs and sex; depression; sleeplessness; nightmares; fatigue; and the like. This is called entity possession, and more and more people are falling victim to it during this period.

Lightbearers are particular targets of entity possession because they tend to be more open at the solar plexus level for want of communicating with the other dimensions. Incoming Sixth Root-Race incarnations are also quite prone to entity possession because their body vehicles are more open to receiving impulses from the higher dimensions. However, as things continue to accelerate, it is becoming more obvious that the general population as a whole can also be at risk, as seen by the growing insanity in society.

Depending on how open the person is to the astral plane, entity possession can start at a young age and be long-standing. Or the possession can be a temporary, random episode. In the case of lightbearers, entity possession is more deliberate, being fostered by the Dark Forces who target lightbearers coming into incarnation in order to disable or veer them off their spiritual missions.

There are three ways we recommend to dispossess yourself of entity attachments.

1. Sound the Om and the Double Om

Astral entities can buzz around you like flies, suggest feelings, ideas and actions that go counter to your mission. These entities know how to calibrate these thoughts to make you think they are your own. Moreover, if they find a willing victim, they can even attach to you. There are three steps to getting rid of the entity disturbance:

1. When you are aware that something is hovering around you, sound the OM orally or silently and most of the time, they will back off. Sounding the OM essentially calls forth your soul to manifest energies that are too high and pure for these entities to withstand. They will leave because they are incompatible with the energies the soul will be emitting through you.

2. Sometimes despite the OM, these entities will manage to stick to you and continue disturbing you. In this case, you can sound the double OM. Essentially, you sound the OM orally or silently. While you are doing this, visualize the ball of light representing your soul that is resident in the pineal gland of your brain. Ask it to sound the OM along with you from there. The result will be your soul and your personality sounding the OM at the same time. But you must be in the process of seeking soul contact to be able to accomplish this. (See Chapter 7)

3. Still sounding the OM orally, visualize the OM energies coming from your soul and cleansing your etheric, astral, and mental bodies. The astral entities should scatter.

2. Invoke Protection from the Spiritual Hierarchy

The Masters of Wisdom and the Angelic realm stand ready to help all those who invoke their guidance and protection. Because of their ever respect for the cosmic law of Free Will, you must invoke their protection. Below is an invocation that may help you rid yourself of these attachments through divine intervention.

INVOCATION FOR PROTECTION:

Beloved Angels of God,
Beloved Masters of Wisdom, Peace and Love,
Beloved Lady Masters of Heaven,
Beloved Elder Brother, Jesus the Christ,
Beloved mighty St. Germain,
Beloved Heavenly Father and Mother
Who are in heaven as on earth,
We come before You
Asking for your heavenly help
In all things that we do.

We ask for your holy protection always
So that the work we are meant to do in this world
Will not be disrupted or delayed in any way,
But will proceed with
The greatest of ease, peace, and blessings.

We are grateful for all the Good
We have been able to do by Your Grace up until now.
And so we come asking for further protection
At all times and in all situations
So that we can continue to serve the Will of God.

We call for round-the-clock protection
Around our homes and the places that we work, eat, and
play.
We call for solid protection
Around our loved ones at all times as well,
That they can never be used as pawns or tools of darkness
Which is only ignorance of God's Love.

Keep us always in the brightest Light.
Keep us immune to the negative pulls
Of the planets, people, or spirits.
Keep us happy and seeing the Truth in every situation,
And free of judgments against our brethren.

And keep us always alert to potential dangers
Coming from any source whatsoever,
Whether seen or unseen,
Known or unknown,
Embodied or disembodied.

And may we always have an avenue
Of escape from danger or mishap
Whenever necessary.

Let us truly be instruments of the Divine,
Seeing clearly what would be
The best course of action to take, if any,
In every situation that we see.

Speak words of wisdom
And counsel into our listening ears
And see to it that we are always surrounded
By angels of light, protection, wisdom and love.
Let us truly reflect

The Presence of God
On earth as it is in Heaven.

See to it that our lives are filled with
Laughter, joy, and love always.
And may we be empowered to bring
These same blessings into the lives of
All those we contact.
Let healings occur in our presence
And miracles, too.

Lord Michael before, Lord Michael behind
Lord Michael to the right, Lord Michael to the left
Lord Michael above, Lord Michael below
Lord Michael, Lord Michael wherever I go.
I AM, its love protecting here!
I AM, its love protecting here!
I AM, its love protecting here![28]

3. Request Telepathic Healing Help

If entity possession has been lodged in your person for some time and you are just discovering that your physical symptoms of say, depression or obsession, may be due to this attachment, you may not feel strong enough to dislodge it by the sounding of the OM. Trained telepathic healers of the Sanctus Germanus Foundation stand ready to help you dispossess these entities without charge.

---

[28] Through trance medium Arthur Pacheco

Just Contact:

telepathichealing@sanctusgermanus.net

Create a Refuge from Distraction

Noise and distractions are the most effective tools the Dark Forces have to prevent you from thinking. To help you gain control over your mind you must try your best to create a thoughtful and contemplative environment around you. If you live with other family members who do not share your spiritual endeavours, try to set up a corner in your house that is sacred to you alone and where you can repair to in order to center yourself and regain control over your mind. If you work in a bustling office, find a spot in the building where you can repair to in order to gift yourself a few moments of quiet and contemplation during the day. If you have a door to your office, close it from time to time and sit quietly. If you are stuck in traffic, use that precious time alone in the car to regain your concentration and center. In other words, recognize and take every opportunity to be alone and to apply the 7/7 Breathing exercise or the Seed Thought meditation in order to regain control over your mind.

Value Silence

If you live in an urban setting as most people do, there are artificial noises as opposed to nature's noises everywhere. This is inevitable in areas of dense population. But there is also a manipulative factor in some of this noise, not from the traffic or common street noise, but noise or music that someone has chosen to play for you.

Background Music

Wherever you go these days there is background music being pumped into your ears and then into your subconscious mind. As acceleration ramps up, this background music seems to be getting more urgent, obscene and violent, in line with the music being played over the pop music radio stations. In shopping centres, restaurants, supermarkets, trains, planes, airports and other public spaces where people congregate, this music is being pumped into your brain and their insidious messages registered subconsciously. If you listen closely and analyze the background music feeding your subconscious mind, you would be astounded. We will discover a range of emotions conveyed in the music such as nostalgia, anger, violence, sex, gender conflicts, marital infidelity, betrayals, broken promises and contracts—all conveyed in repetitive and low level chords or rhythms intended to stimulate the lower chakras and anchor the human being in lower bestial emotions and actions.

One of the techniques of mind manipulation is repetition. The subconscious mind responds to repetition and if you listen to the "lyrics" in today's pop music you will note that there is little logic, wit or poetic value. Instead there are one or two catch phrases that are repeated over and over to a repetitive beat. Observe how many people sitting in a café reading, chatting or working on a laptop, nod their heads to the beat of the music in the background. They have unfortunately been drawn into the magnetic repetition and beat of the music, and it is highly likely that their subconscious minds have absorbed the mindless and negative thought-forms which will manifest sometime in the future in corresponding action or emotions.

This is not innocent background music, but messages that have been chosen to convey and reinforce certain base human personality characteristics upon the subconscious mind, with the main message "This is what you are, and this is where you'll stay."

Other music is intended to give you a momentary "feel good" high to make you buy more products in the store, while certain hip music is designed to make you feel hip and buy the hip fashions. It all boils down to base mind manipulation, and if you are one of the victims of lengthy exposure to the sheep-inducing rays of television, you will easily fall prey to these forms of mental manipulation. If you are easily manipulated by the commercial use of background music, you are also a ready victim of political manipulation.

Background Radio

Unlike the background music in a shopping mall, noise from radios is a choice. You switch it on or switch it off. Active listening to programs of choice is one thing, for your conscious mind in actively filtering out the lies for the truth. However, if you fall asleep or are busy working on something, then the radio becomes background noise infiltrating your subconscious mind without any conscious filtering. The radio in the background begins to play the same role of unconscious mind manipulation. Turn off the radio when you are not concentrating on the program content and actively listening.

Turn off the Television

If there is one simple positive thing you could do for yourself to help you survive the turmoil today, it would be to unplug the television set and junk it. Television ramps up emotions through sound, breaks down your thought defences and causes your mind to be less discerning. Furthermore, reinforced by deliberate programming, it stimulates your emotional astral body and makes you susceptible to the agitated astral waves on the astral plane that govern the tenor of the world's mass consciousness.

The Spiritual Hierarchy has already warned us that the electronic rays emanating from the television screen numb the brain, making discernment almost impossible. We have pointed out this stark fact in Volume 1, and how millions have become sheep by watching television. To keep one's mental independence, you must break any dependence on the television set. The television is not your friend and should not be used to make up for your sense of loneliness, isolation or boredom. Rather than entertaining you, it will enslave you mentally.

Without the television chanting pre-programmed emotions and panic, your mental abilities are better able to discern and evaluate information spread through the media including the Internet. The discerning mind can distinguish between lies and the bits of truth seeping through the lies and can be used to take rational action when times of real crisis reach your doorsteps.

Keeping up with World and Local Events

Cutting yourself off from world events and resting in ignorance of the world's events is not an option for the lightbearer.   What is necessary is to develop the ability to reinterpret the news by seeing through the manipulation in order to discern truth from the lies. Keep up with the news by reading reputable magazines and newspapers or news sites on the internet.   The Internet gives you the choice of what and when to read in order to keep informed.   So strike a balance between keeping yourself informed about events around you and shielding yourself from mass mind manipulation that would pull you away from your centre.

If you meditate regularly and are working toward soul contact, certain news items will jump out at you and stick in your mind as reasonable.   Highly emotional events should be recognized for what they are, and you must make a conscious decision to turn off the radio or television and reject whatever is being paraded before you. It is better to choose and read what you deem is important using the internet rather than sit in front of the television set and allow whoever has programmed the evening of shows to dominate your life.   Most of all, turn it off and learn to value silence.

Conclusion

The ability to take control of your mind is essential in order to navigate through this period. A mind that is subject to the vagaries of the astral plane and Dark Force subliminal mind manipulation will be at the beck and call of your emotional body which will whipsaw you along with the waves of fear and panic. You will feel helpless and directionless.

What we have proposed above will help you navigate through this transition, for these methods have stood the test of time throughout other world crises. They are not gimmicked with present-day pop psychology, herb supplements or promises to upgrade your DNA. These methods are simply based on the all-powerful "God Within".

Chapter 7

Implementing Your Soul Plan

After you have regained control over your mind through better concentration, the next step is to seek soul contact with that part of the Great Amon Ra that is your "God Within". Your life's purpose in the current turmoil will become more apparent. Most lightbearers know deep down that they have a mission to fulfill but many go through life distracted and unable to define what that mission is. When the soul is able to express itself clearly through your physical vehicle, you will march through the turmoil knowing your purpose and the reason you chose to incarnate during this period. You will also be led to the resources that will enable you to carry out your mission.

Tuning into your Soul Plan

Establishing soul contact is the single most important life-changing experience you will undertake in this incarnation. However, closer contact with your soul will also demand changes to your physical and spiritual life that you may resist or be too afraid to carry out. This is where many lightbearers fail. Then again, you may also be ripe for soul contact and can rejoice in the fruits and wisdom that such contact can bring into your life and be willing to make all the necessary adjustments to your life to fulfill your mission.

As lightbearers you have incarnated during this period to help the world transition into the New Age. The role you play in this whole scenario is part of a multi-pieced puzzle that makes up earth's Divine Plan. Although you and your spiritual masters elaborated your individual plan, when you incarnated on earth, you did so totally blind to this mission. Your job was to live through all the experiences you had planned and at the right moment lift the veil on your individual plan and implement it in concert with thousands of other lightbearers. Together all the individual plans would honeycomb together in a particular geographical area and serve as regional divine plans. All the regional plans would concord with the whole divine plan for earth.

"Seek and Ye Shall Find"

If you feel deep inside that you have a mission for being on earth that needs to be fulfilled before you end your incarnation, then you must lift the veil that obscures your individual plan and perceive it as it is written in your soul. There are no quick and easy ways to access this soul plan despite promises from New Age charlatans and psychics that they can read your akashic records and even your soul! The only way you can access this soul information is to go deep within yourself through meditation until you contact your soul.

In certain instances initiates of the Spiritual Hierarchy may reveal the first steps of a soul plan to an individual for strategic reasons or to guide him or her back on track. But in general, the seeker must practice the biblical adage: "Seek and ye shall find." The seeker who sincerely digs for this information, disciplining him or herself in the meditation practice is bound to become a more reliable disciple and worker for the Spiritual Hierarchy. Those flitting from medium to medium, teacher to teacher trying to find someone else to define their mission in life are really showing the Spiritual Hierarchy how unreliable they will be if ever they reach the stage of implementing their soul plans. Past experience has shown that the majority of those who were given indications about their soul mission never followed through, allowing daily life concerns instead to absorb them fully.

Method for Soul Contact

We reprint for you the In-Breath meditation method recommended by the Spiritual Hierarchy and which appears on our website www.sanctusgermanus.net and in volume 2 of *The Sanctus Germanus Prophecies.* It comes from the ancient tradition of Raja Yoga and has stood the test of time.

The In-Breath meditation attempts to put your conscious physical self in contact with the soul which resides in the pineal gland in the centre of your head. The distance from your outer body to the pineal gland is minuscule but the journey can be long and arduous and full of obstacles. Therefore, in the first stages, doing the In-Breath Meditation must be an act of conscious will and persistence. Many give up in the beginning, but persistence, as in all human endeavours, will eventually yield its fruits. The adventure and surprises you will experience will be boundless.

The In-Breath Meditation

Meditation, when properly understood, is the stilling of the physical body, generally in a position where the spine is straight and erect, sitting up, not lying down. Your place of meditation should be fairly comfortable as to temperature and somewhere you are likely not to be disturbed by others. An atmosphere of the spirit should be cultivated around it if possible.

When you sit to meditate, you must come to feel that you are about to have a conversation with your God, your Higher Self, and nothing less. You should approach meditation as you approach the altar of invocation--with humility, awe, respect, great love and gratitude. With the proper attitude, approach, and place, we suggest the following meditation procedure:

1. Sit in a comfortable posture with your spine straight and erect. You may sit in the traditional yogi meditation position on the floor or straight up in a comfortable chair.

2. Invoke the Violet Flame of Protection or read the Invocation of Protection in the previous chapter.

3. Begin to breathe deeply and honour the breath that is yours to draw in and to exhale. And with each breath, one should realize that one is drawing in pure life and light. Concentrate in the inhalation and exhalation of the breath.

4. As you breathe deeply, initially focus your attention in the head area, the top of the head in particular. Become aware of your own aura.

5. Then, become aware of your spine, the central beam of the temple of the body, the spinal column, that lovely dimensional doorway into inner space. Focus on the spine as you get used to the rhythm of the breath, as it goes in, as it goes out, and eventually release your attention on the breathing as it continues at the proper pace by itself.

6. Focus all attention on the spinal column itself, holding the attention there. Seek to visualize it as a tube of pure white light.

7. You begin to have the desire to go into it, for it is indeed a doorway. It is a dimensional opening in the physical body to your inner world. You seek to go in it. You must have the desire to go in it, the will to go in, and in, and in. You must will yourself to go in, not unlike one paddling a canoe upstream against the current and not unlike the salmon that doggedly keep swimming upstream against the current that keeps beating them back. But they don't stop. Use your will to go in, in, in.

8. In each session of meditation, at some point you will hit an inner foothold, a landmark, so to speak. You'll

know what it is by the sheer experience of it. If you think you cannot go any deeper, you should keep trying nonetheless until you cannot go any more. At this point, stop and simply enjoy the inner surroundings.

9. Seek to become aware of the inner atmosphere as the breath continues to inhale and exhale at its own steady pace.

10. Seek to know yourself as you are, beyond thoughts, feelings, sensations and certainly physical bodies. Every session will be a new adventure and a continuation of your journey inward.

11. Seek to know that part of you that has never changed and shall never change, the part of you that is eternal. Seek to feel your own endlessness.

This may seem like a very cursory and basic approach to meditation but we assure you that if properly followed, it will lead you to inner breakthroughs of the type that most people so much want to experience but are so unaware of how to.

In-Breath Meditation in a Group Setting

We have stated in Volume 2 that guided meditation[29] is a form of mind manipulation, no matter how good the intentions of the person doing the guiding. It can lead to dependence on a recording or a person and thus does not

---

[29] One person orally leading a meditation.

develop the conscious will and discipline necessary to sit down and meditate. Meditation is essentially an individual action. So do the meditation yourself rather than in a guided situation or with the help of psychics or mediums.

If the In-Breath Meditation is done in a group setting, let silence reign so that each person can meditate according to his or her abilities. Let no one person guide the meditation. Again, this is an individual journey and no one can know the soul better than you, for it is the real you.

If the In-Breath Meditation is combined with a seed thought, let each one meditate on the thought once entry into one's inner world is achieved. Whatever enlightened perspective your meditation yields regarding this seed thought can then be transferred to the mass consciousness from where it will be shared with those open to such thoughts. In this way the results of your meditation can be shared in a group.

Light in the Head

When you perceive a soft light in the head even when your eyes are closed in a dark room, you have reached the realm of your inner prelate, the soul. This soft light will get brighter as your soul is allowed full liberation of expression through your physical vehicle. This is the essence of Soul Liberation.

Developing Discernment

Developing spiritual discernment is a major outcome of this meditation. If there is too much emotional yearning and desire for soul contact, astral entities, posing as guides or Masters, will quickly jump in and mislead you. This may take place at the beginning of your meditation experience as you are adjusting to the In-Breath Meditation and is one of the most difficult phases leading to soul contact. Ignore these voices and continue your journey inward. You will learn to walk the fine line of spiritual discernment and better distinguish between the false and the true through experience.

Your journey into your inner world is very similar to walking down a busy street. Would you allow the first stranger to come up to you and advise you on personal matters? As you journey through your emotional or astral body, you may also access a crowd of entities jockeying for your attention. Chatter, voices, substance-less advice saying nothing new--all these are signs of communicating with the dimension just over the line called death. Just because they are invisible does not mean they are spiritual. They are just made up of slightly higher vibratory matter. Do exactly as you would do on the earth, don't listen to them and continue your breathing until it takes you into the core of your inner world where you will be safe from these extraneous influences.

Moreover, the Master Kuthumi suggests that it may be your own self which poses the obstacles and offers this advice while you journey inward:

. . .(W)hen you "enter into the Heart of Silence—where you commune with your own God-Self, . . be extremely wise, alert and careful of the response that you will receive first of all from your own bodies because you are a complex mechanism—a seven-fold being. Now, whereas the glory of . . . your Causal Body and your Holy Christ Self can never lead you astray—your lower bodies have voice, consciousness and intelligence of their own—and these voices, this consciousness and this intelligence within them endeavours often to serve its own selfish ends through you.

. . . Know always that the prompting which builds up the personality, that which gives aggrandizement to the human ego, is not the "Still Small Voice" of the Presence, but rather the etheric rumblings of your own past experiences, the emotional desires of your feeling world, or mental concepts and precepts from your past lives.

. . . As you proceed into an understanding of The Voice of the Silence, know that that which makes you humble, that which makes you loving, that which makes you pure, that which makes you harmonious, is of God. The feelings that stir within your heart that desire to make of this Star a Planet of Light, to relieve the burden of your fellowman, to raise those in pain and distress into understanding and harmony—that is of Light. That which decreases the personality and increases the Power of Christ—that is of God![30]

Study the Ancient Wisdom to help you discern the quality of the substance being conveyed to you. Experienced and trained interlocutors of the Spiritual Hierarchy, such as Gautama Buddha, Jesus, St. Germain, and countless avatars, have brought forth the Ancient Wisdom. These are the true esoteric teachings from the Brotherhood of Light.

Deeply steeping yourself in the age-old Wisdom will help you gain a sense of the quality and nature of communications from the Great Brotherhood of Light and help you distinguish them from those of astral entities and spurious modern-day teachings and sophism. The latter is full of sweet talk to draw you into its influence and usually repetitions of information widely circulated on the internet and basically vacuous. So developing discernment in this instance is basically learning the difference between astral voices and soul impulses and intuitions.

Some lightbearers report difficulties in doing the In-Breath Meditation or any meditation for that matter. We offer no consolation but suggest persistence. It is true that this meditation takes a conscious effort to work your way into your inner world. But unfortunately, no one else can meditate for you. It can only be done if you make a conscious decision to do it and then follow

---

[30] Printz, Thomas ed. (Master Morya) *The First Ray*, Ascended Master Teaching Foundation, Mount Shasta, California: 1986, pp 103-104

through by persistently meditating daily until soul contact has been made. These times call for persistence and discipline rather than coddling.

Moreover, your persistence confirms a commitment to your mission on earth.

The Path Leading to the Soul Unfolds

Your soul plan is revealed step by step and never all at once. Once you fulfill one step, you will first have to take the next step before more will be revealed--this to test your commitment and sincerity to follow through with the soul impulses that you are receiving. A Path fraught with challenges and obstacles awaits you, but the rewards are so much greater.

How to Distinguish Between Soul and Astral Impulses

In the latter part of the well-known book, *The Initiate*, by Cyril Scott, there is an allegory of the initiate's path and the obstacles and temptations that appear along the path to hinder the initiate's quest. Today the path to soul unfoldment involves not only physical encounters but discarnate ones as well.

On your path to implement your soul plan, you will encounter many situations that may sidetrack or mislead you. Astral entities posing as masters or angelic beings will appear using familiar spiritual terms that appeal to the lightbearer's good intentions, such as healing, helping others, or grander schemes of world salvation. These, of course, play upon the natural tendencies of the lightbearer but they can also be used to trick you and most of the time, ruin you both morally and financially.

Rushing and urgent action is a sign of astrally inspired activity and can lead to aimless actions that often times whipsaw people hither and yond and eventually off the path. In contrast, the impulses of soul are calm, deliberate and come from "knowing".

A lightbearer managed to sell her home just before the housing market crashed and realized a good profit. Her "guides" urgently pushed her to purchase another house in another state and invest in a piece of desert property that supposedly could serve as a dimensional portal for the healing centre she always dreamed of setting up.

From a practical point of view, this guidance was disastrous. The state where she chose to purchase her new home turned out to be one of the hardest hit in the economic downturn. In a matter of one year, the value of her new house dropped by one-half and her new mortgage soon exceeded the value of the house. She is now bankrupt, and the property that was to become her healing centre has been seized. This is an example of how dodgy "guides" in the astral plane can mislead and ruin lightbearers. It is also an example of the lightbearer's lack of discernment or the ability to distinguish between good and bad information coming from discarnate guides.

Sending away false discarnate guides may also pose a problem. On one hand, they are not likely to leave voluntarily but could morph into other identities offering you assistance against the very one you might be chasing away. If you accept this assistance, you will be doubly entangled in their web of deception. So beware of these foxes in sheep's clothing offering you assistance. On the other hand, the lightbearer may not want to let go of the discarnate guides even if the guidance is erroneous. Some guides have hovered around the person for years, providing both good and bad information, stoking the person's ego and even providing "friendship" to a lonely heart. Since they can see better into the future, they know how to set you up for the kill at the right moment. In the above case, the astral guide could see the looming real estate crisis and led our lightbearer right into it.

In another case, a psychic advised another lightbearer that he should purchase a home in a neighbouring state immediately as it was to fulfill his spiritual mission. Guided to a listing on the Internet, both the medium and the lightbearer rushed to the site only to find a dilapidated building that needed thousands of dollars of work and was haunted to boot! The medium desperately tried to recoup his credibility by rushing to a nearby broker to find another property in the same town. "This is the one," he declared pointing to another listing, "it has a better dimensional portal. It comes down through the chimney, all the way to the basement. It would be perfect for your healing mission." Happily by this time the lightbearer woke up and declared the whole house-hunting episode and the medium a total fraud.

Implementing a soul impulse or guidance "on the rush" should throw up the red flags. The rush or urgency is designed to negate any logical or rational thinking and plunge you into a path that will veer you off track and ultimately ruin or disable you.

As we mentioned above, your soul mission is never revealed to you in full but in bits and pieces, primarily because you might become too overwhelmed to fulfill it or run the other way because some fundamental changes in your life are required. Each step tests your commitment and reliability to your plan and each step is met with adequate resources to realize it. This is important because too many lightbearers say they want to do this and that as part of their plan but don't have the money to realize it. Experience has shown that if the resources are not available, then perhaps you are not on the right track in realizing your soul plan. At this point, you should stop and honestly take stock of what you are doing. Have you turned your path into a moneymaking venture? Is your motivation divine service or just promoting yourself? Is your outward modesty but a façade of greater ambitions to become famous or yet another guru?

Meditate and seek more guidance from your soul, for that is where the plan is. Try another avenue that would accomplish the same objective. Just know that many roads lead to Rome and there is not just one way to accomplish a soul plan objective.

This brings up another important subject and that is free will. The soul plan suggests objectives and gives you the option to choose how you are to accomplish them. It never says "Buy this property for this price or get this financing." You are operating on the earth plane and hopefully through your life's many experiences have learned how to negotiate your way through life in dense matter. The Spiritual Hierarchy needs workers who can make these basic decisions on the earth plane, otherwise what use are you as their arms and feet on earth? You must practice common sense and use sound business principles to navigate your way through this maya. Rushing, as we said, is the best tactic to derail you. So take your time and evaluate your next step according to rational and sound business practices.

"Guides" prompted a lightbearer to set up an esoteric bookstore in a resort town. Yet instead of locating the store in the centre of activity that would afford him adequate foot traffic and exposure to the public, he was "guided" to purchase store space in an isolated location on the outskirts of the town centre. He said he was divinely guided there. But from a logical, business point of view such a location made no sense. As a consequence, the bookstore is bankrupt, and a valuable resource for the spiritual community will be lost.

So how do you know that you are receiving a soul impulse as opposed to an astral one? A genuine soul impulse is non-emotional. It does not involve tears of joy or adoration. It is a deep knowing, which is a logical consequence of where you have come from in life. If you have been trained as a lawyer, for instance, it is unlikely that your soul calling will lead you to become an auto mechanic and vice versa. Nevertheless, your calling may require a change in your life style or location, but the deep knowing keeps you moving forward in the right direction. There is no rush or urgency, and there is usually time to think rationally about the next step and plan it out correctly. Moreover the resources are made available for you to carry out the next step, provided you take the first step.

Tough Decisions

Soul contact will prompt you to take action with ample time to prepare. Sometimes this may mean disrupting your present life, even uprooting your family, much to their objections. A lightbearer lamented that although he felt a strong urge to move to one of the Spiritual Regions, he could not move because he would have to leave his friends and neighbours, and the kids would have to change schools.

Another lightbearer is quite clear that she must move out of a low-lying coastal area. But her husband thinks moving based on her soul promptings is ridiculous, especially since there are no job prospects where they would move to, and they both have good paying jobs where they are presently.

This is a tough decision. She must decide for herself what is more important in this lifetime: her soul mission or her husband's reasoning. If she follows her soul impulses, they would move first, then the rest of the plan would unfold. But if everything must be mapped out for them—a steady job, nice house, right schools for the kids etc.—all guaranteed, they will never move. This is not how the Spiritual Hierarchy works. The Spiritual Hierarchy wants to know how sincere and reliable your commitment is to follow through on your mission first. So nothing will happen without taking the first step.

Once you take the first step you will be quite surprised how things unfold according to your soul plan. But the first step is a wholesale leap of faith that many lightbearers are unwilling to take. The result is mental turmoil and contradiction until it builds up to frustration and finally to an explosive situation where the decision must be made. Going against your soul plan can also lead one to depression and ultimately insane behaviour because you are essentially being torn in opposite directions. The personality wars with the soul, or to put it in ancient biblical terms, the flesh wars against the spirit. You either resolve this problem by making a firm decision and living with its consequences or you battle the contradiction within yourself until you are forced to come to a decision to maintain your sanity.

This problem exposes a fundamental misconception among some lightbearers. Their original missions have been put on the back burner while their mortal lives have become so important that what they have forgotten or refuse to admit what they came here to do for the Spiritual Hierarchy. In other words, risking the two cars, the swimming pool and the good material life becomes more important than helping humanity's transit into the New Age. Once they end this incarnation they will return to face the music: "Mission Unaccomplished".

Another lightbearer also got the impulse to move out of a low-lying coastal area. When a recent hurricane devastated part of her city, she took it as a stark reminder and confirmation that her soul impulse was correct. Her husband has a business in town, so he does not want to move. Yet she has decided nonetheless that she will

197

move to one of the Spiritual Regions even if she has to do it alone and has announced her intentions to all around her. This is the kind of tough decision a lightbearer must take, for what lies ahead in this transition will not be a picnic.

By maintaining her intentions to carry through with her soul plans, things have miraculously unfolded. Her husband sold his troubled business and other assets that would have tied them to their present location, and now they are free to relocate.

Resistance to many lightbearers' plans comes most vehemently from their closest family members, primarily spouses. Understandably, their family's well-being weighs most heavily on their minds, even at the expense of their soul plans. This is why it takes strength and fortitude to move in the direction of one's soul even if it goes against the common thread, i.e. your family considerations.

Many will be the reasons for abandoning your soul plan and it mostly boils down to placing too great an importance on your mortal life on this earth plane rather than on the greater mission you were sent here to do. It takes guts and grit to break with these impediments and fulfill one's mission.

Most lightbearers who have made the tough decisions and who are pursuing their missions move forward steadily and silently without recourse to publicity and promises of fame. Others have mistakenly commercialized their missions into moneymaking schemes, providing spiritual entertainment for the shaky uncommitted ones who flit from venue to venue in search of an easier way out instead of full commitment to service. This search of the uncommitted, the proverbial fence sitter, has provided ready fodder for unscrupulous "spiritual" schemes, therapies, life coaching, quick-fix solutions and fast track seminars and workshops to enlightenment. It is the proverbial "blind leading the blind", and conjures up thoughts that the moneychangers in the temple have returned to take full advantage of this situation.

Implementing your soul plan step-by-step and knowing that you are headed in the right direction is probably the most fulfilling activity you will ever undertake in this incarnation, for it is the primary purpose for your being here. You will feel happy and satisfied, and all the resources you need to fulfill your mission will come into your life. It is only logical that when you drew up your mission plan before this incarnation, you also wrote into it the resources you would need to carry out this plan. Would you have drawn up a plan that would have left you high and dry without resources?

Indeed as with all wonderful endeavours taking place in the duality on the earth plane, there will always be obstacles on the path. Overcoming them just builds even stronger character and commitment.

Some Advice to Young Adults on Marriage

Experience has shown that one of the main obstacles to pursuing the Path of your mission is a spouse who is not in accord with your spiritual concerns. If you discover your mission after you have a family, your spouse may be your principal opposition to any changes to the status quo. His or her opposition can be vociferous, mocking, or deadly silent. In some situations, two spouses can come to an agreement so that one does not outwardly oppose the other. This could be characterised as silent opposition. In any case, the lightbearer is placed in an almost intolerable situation being torn in opposite directions or being forced to carry out as best he or she can his or her mission in secret. Some lightbearers have even left their spouses and families to be able to fulfill their missions.

Our advice to younger lightbearers contemplating marriage is to first define as best you can, your mission on earth before getting married. One young man cried, "I've got a beautiful girlfriend, a good job, a nice apartment. I've traveled far and wide and I still feel something is missing! What's wrong?" Arriving at this point, it is time to take stock of where you are in fulfilling your divine mission. But this is also the time NOT to get married.

Once your mission becomes clearer in your conscious mind and you have hurdled the testing and trials, by the Law of Attraction you should begin running into people of the same ilk and could even meet that right partner on the path who would not only understand your mission but enhance it.

The Ancient Egyptian Master Serapis Bey offers this advice:

Know, O Brother mine, that where a truly spiritual love seeks to consolidate itself doubly by a pure, permanent union of the two, in its earthly sense, it commits no sin, no crime in the eyes of the great Ain-Soph, for it is but the divine repetition of the Male and Female Principles—the microcosmic reflection of the first condition of Creation. On such a union angels may well smile! But they are rare, Brother mine, and can only be created under the wise and loving supervision of the Lodge, in order that the sons and daughters of clay might not be utterly degenerated, and the Divine Love of the Inhabitants of Higher Spheres (Angels) towards the daughters of Adam be repeated. But even such must suffer, before they are rewarded. Man's Atma may remain pure and as highly spiritual while it is united with its material body; why should not two souls in two bodies remain as pure and uncontaminated notwithstanding the earth passing union of the latter two.[31]

As long as you are not on the right path, the sense of mission will nag you throughout your whole life. And if you have already committed to a spouse and children, you should fulfill your obligations to them as promised. You will either have to compromise your time and effort to your mission (and thus be proven less reliable) or you may have to exit this incarnation without fulfilling your

---

[31] Quoted from Letter 19 circa 1875 from the Master Serapis Bey to Henry Steel Olcott in *The Story of the Mahatma Letters,* by C. Jinarajadasa, The Theosophical Publishing House: Adyar, Madras, 1977.

mission. If your calling is so strong, then you must work out a situation with your spouse that allows you to fulfill your mission and keep your obligations to your family. Unfortunately, there are few options in between fulfilling or not fulfilling your mission, as the Spiritual Hierarchy does not compromise on quality or commitment of its lightbearers.

Partnerships with Others

Partnering with others who are not on the Path in order to implement your soul plan can cause untold problems. The most obvious differences concern basic morals and your need to compromise your principles. Just because someone is psychically inclined does not mean he or she is on the Path. The worst type of partner would be one who is led by the nose by astral "guides" posing as higher beings. In this situation, you have the makings of sabotage through misleading information, bad decisions, laziness, hidden agendas, back-handed betrayals and a host of other basic moral issues.

Marriage and Spousal Opposition

In the above section we covered this situation as it applies to young adults before they get married. But what if, you are a "late bloomer" and late in your marriage, you discover your spiritual mission which puts you in direct opposition with your spouse and the obligations you have toward your family? This is quite a thorny question and a situation that many lightbearers find themselves in today.

An understanding spouse who is open-minded enough not to oppose your mission and does not pose any outward opposition would be the ideal. Sometimes you and your spouse may have such similar thoughts that you both can pursue a common mission. This is possible but quite rare as the Master Serapis so put it. And you can never force your spouse to believe in what you hold true and vice versa.

There are also lightbearers who secretly work on their mission without their spouses knowing. Those who are trapped in marriages that do not allow them to outwardly express and fulfill their missions must obviously compromise or justify their situation by doing little permissible things that make them think they are on track. However, such a situation is not in the spirit of soul liberation which is in this case is imprisoned by marriage and will eventually explode.

In some, the calling becomes so strong that they can no longer compromise their mission, and they take the very strong measure of separating themselves from the marriage to fulfill it.

It all boils down to choosing what is most important to you. There is no right or wrong way. You live and adjust to whatever decision you make, the consequences of which you will have to face either on this plane or in the higher dimensions when you exit.

Money and Security

The question of money and security remains paramount in some lightbearers' minds. This is understandable in the world we live in, and a poverty-prone lightbearer can hardly fulfill his or her mission adequately if overly concerned by the lack of money. Some lightbearers have solved this problem by earning enough through their regular jobs, occupations or investments to be able to devote their time to divine service, for divine service must be given freely and unselfishly. Some, for karmic reasons, may not find the financial freedom they would like and thus must adjust their soul implementation to what they are able to do. The Master Morya states:

All of you today suffer from such obligatory karma. Those of you who do not have financial freedom, one day had much wealth to incorporate in God's plan and withheld it or used it freely for personal pleasures. . . .Now when you would serve, there is neither that peace nor direction which you feel is essential to your success. None may cry that they 'would if they could.' Forgive you, each one for the limitations that make you less pliable instruments in Our hands now that your heart desires to serve![32]

---

[32] El Morya (Thomas Printz Ed.), *The First Ray*, Ascended Master Teaching Foundation, Mt. Shasta, California: 1986 , p. 78

Temptation to Commercialize Your Soul Plan

Some lightbearers delude themselves into thinking that as part of their service to humanity they can charge fees or make a living out of it. To be in service to the Spiritual Hierarchy, you should not expect to enrich yourself, as this contradicts the notion of selfless divine service. Do you consider your work for the Brotherhood a job? Are you seeking employment and money through divine service?

New age businesses often justify their sometimes exorbitant fees as compensation for balancing the energies they expend, i.e. tit for tat. This has led some to offer services as "Masters" of a particular therapy after spending tuition for a weekend training course. This is not service but the blind leading the blind and New Age chicanery.

Indeed, covering expenses that are incurred for providing a service is one thing but profiting monetarily from such service is highly questionable. Does this not contradict the very notion of selfless service?

The Master Morya advises the following on this controversial issue:

> The principle of life is that when an individual dedicates himself to becoming a Teacher of the Law, if his motive is to spread the light, and not to make a living, We immediately enfold such a one in Our protection and guidance. We would like such sincere hearts to have an opportunity to unfold in a place of beauty . . . and someday this shall be.

The implication here is that the Masters will protect and guide those who dedicate their lives to service rather than trying to make a living out of it.   When money is the hidden motive, and we might add the promotion of self also, there is a tendency to compromise your values. You find yourself generating activities, proposing consultations, offering therapies, teaching classes in order to generate more funds to pay the bills instead of in the spirit of selfless service.   Or when the ego takes over, you find yourself promoting yourself instead of the Divine Laws and teachings.   If the service is offered with a genuine heart and pure motives then the resources and money will flow toward you in many unpredictable ways.

The Return of the Money Changers to the Temple

The Bible tells of the Master Jesus' rampage through the temple to expel the moneychangers.   During this period of acceleration, the moneychangers have returned in full force.   Schemes touting secret knowledge of certain cosmic laws (that have been known to mankind since time immemorial) have been packaged and commercialized to cater to selfish wants and desires. The organizers use mass marketing techniques bordering on evangelical hysteria to draw people into expensive seminars, spa packages, exclusive cruises and mass conferences—all of which are couched to "help one's neighbour" or more honestly enrich oneself.   Famous media people use their influence to endorse these schemes, thus amplifying the numbers exposed to these schemes.   The duped are often left with credit card debts beyond their ability to repay or become cynical and disappointed toward the cosmic law that has not worked to fulfill their selfish desires.

Purveyors of "feel good" fill the pages of New Age publications in countries around the world. Massage therapies, vitamin and natural supplements, chakra cleansings, reiki therapy, spas, DNA upgrades, divine energy boosts for increased sexual prowess, ET contact for superhuman performance, psychic development seminars and the latest therapy of the month . . . all point to the circus of money changers who are back in the temple! All involve paying someone to do something to you to make you feel better.

One main lesson we can learn from the "feel good" wave is that it is yet another Dark Force strategy to appeal to the emotional body which acceleration is agitating, especially among lightbearers and other energy-sensitive individuals. Through these moneymaking schemes, the agitation is only temporarily calmed, and people willingly pay a lot for this temporary reprieve. Very often the lightbearer is veered off his or her path of soul plan implementation, because many of these schemes are couched in spiritual terms. Many lightbearers have been among those misled and must find their way back to the Path of selfless service.

Those targeted or misled are the very incarnations that were meant to combat the Dark Forces rather than become their victims. Thus, as the war between Light and darkness continues, those who fall victim to these schemes must pick themselves up and re-evaluate their motives before they can rejoin the forces of light. Being waylaid in such a manner can only weaken the effort to build enough light to combat the Dark Forces but one that has been severely tested by these schemes should hopefully make for an even strong lightbearer.

ET Intrusion

Another tactic being used to steer lightbearers off the path is the appearance of extraterrestrial federations promising help to mankind during these times of turmoil. The lightbearer is often assigned a military rank such as a colonel or general (all chiefs and no Indians) who will lead an intergalactic war against the Dark Forces. They promise to remake one's DNA to empower people during these times of turmoil. This may make a fine script for Star Wars, but when we really take a good look at what this tactic is trying to accomplish, we realize this is an attempt to stage a coup against earth's Spiritual Hierarchy in violation of cosmic law.

Using the glamour of self-importance and rank, lightbearers come under the influence of those who do not belong on the earth and thus would not know how to solve problems on earth. Those who lead us into a New Age on earth must be the tried and true of the earth experience, not extra-terrestrials from another planet or solar system who promise a magic wand solution to earthly matters!

Shamanism and Lemurian Inspired Practices

Shamanism and Lemurian-inspired practices such as ho'oponopono, drumming (a form of sound hypnosis), and trance healing are plainly ancient practices of the Third Root-Race and are not applicable to incarnations of the Fifth Root-Race and the incoming Sixth Root-Race. The present fascination with these practices is all the more surprising in that they seem to have been resurrected despite mankind having evolved through millennia of the Fourth Root-Race (the Atlanteans). Are we to believe that these ancient practices of a bygone evolution of mankind dating millions of years ago will lead us into the New Age? If this were true, what does this say about the process of evolution?

There are no subterranean Lemurian cities connected to the Master St. Germain buried in the mountains as some imagine. These are purely astral inventions that surviving astral shells of Lemurian throwbacks project onto dodgy, untrained psychics who think they are communicating with higher spiritual dimensions buried in the core of the earth. In one breath they spout off the "I AM" teachings and in the next they burrow beneath to the earth's surface to worship subterranean beings. Is there no end to this insanity? Anyone thinking that their soul plan includes such practices is being grossly misled. Let us turn our gaze upward to our "God Within".

Reliability of the Lightbearer Must Be Proven

Implied in the trials and tribulations you will encounter on the path to fulfilling your soul mission are the numerous tests of your reliability. As a lightbearer you most likely belong to an ashram of a Master located on the upper mental plane. Initiates of your Master's ashram have been assigned to remind you of your soul plan to determine your reliability and commitment first before more can be revealed to you. Reliability, consistency and persistence are all qualities the Spiritual Hierarchy look for. Your soul is in complete accord to test your personality for these qualities in order to prepare it for divine service.

First and foremost, you must adhere to the basic morals of the society. You cannot expect the Spiritual Hierarchy to consider you reliable if you are a white collar thief, dishonest, or hooked on drugs. It would be unreasonable to think that the Masters would be that magnanimous! They would continue to love you for who you really are as soul but would consider you unreliable as one of their "runners" doing the grunt work on the earth plane.

Second, you will be thoroughly tested for your real motives to serve. Even if you are leading a moral life, do not expect the Masters to swoop down and entrust you with occult secrets or assignments without putting you through many tests and trials. Many people may cross your path and offer you distractions that are quite attractive from a material sense. Some may offer you money, services or conveniences to gain entrance into your good graces then mislead you. You must objectively evaluate these offers and meditate on their validity to determine if they are genuinely part of the divine plan. If they are not, then turn them away, no matter how juicy the offer, and how much you need the money.

The lightbearer must examine his or her motives with a great deal of honesty. The Masters must test every single one of your motives. Are you working for them with a hidden agenda that seeks monetary compensation, fame, or recognition? Are you really looking to become a spiritual guru who can attract many adherents so you can enrich yourself? Moreover, are you promoting yourself instead of the truth or the divine plan? Do you easily fall victim to flattery from the astral plane and thus submit to its prompting?

Further Help from Your Spiritual Ashram and Master

Each lightbearer belongs to an ashram of a Master. But just because you have psychic abilities does not mean you can invoke a Master's appearance. They will contact you, not the other way round. You have developed a relationship with your Master over countless lifetimes, and the Master knows your soul inside and out. If this incarnation falls short of your and their expectations, they may use other means to awaken you back on the Path. This could be direct contact through physical appearance or vivid dreams. So on very, very rare occasions, a Master may materialize to communicate something important or to drive home a point.

One lightbearer sighed, "If only I could meet a Master face to face, then maybe I would know my soul purpose." Would he really? Would he take the steps needed to implement his soul plan or would he have other pre-conditions for doing so?   Past experience has shown that even when such direct intervention has been used, the "success rate" of awakening has been low.

For quite a long period the Spiritual Hierarchy used the manifestation of phenomena to catch people's attention, especially through the Spiritualist movement. People then became fixed or obsessed with the phenomenon instead of their soul purposes!   For this reason, it was decided that if the lightbearer were motivated enough to dig deep into the soul for the answers, a higher "success rate" could possibly be achieved.   The Master St. Germain once stated:

> (I came) so that each one of you would really know
> That there is such a thing as phenomena.
> It isn't always apports
> And it isn't always smoke
> That issues out of a medium's throat
> But instead it's that thing that can turn a bloke
> Into one who's heaven's fires doth stoke. . .
> Through Her love or His great, great devotion![33]

It is astounding how some psychics or mediums will organize venues and claim to call forth the Masters to provide spiritual entertainment for an audience on a boring winter's evening.   You cannot invoke a Master to come and entertain a group of people.   Nor can you sell tickets for such an occasion. This is a gross misuse and

---

[33]   From   the   Master's   "Welcome   Message"   on www.sanctusgermanus.net

disrespect of these marvelous and advanced beings. And since they will not be used in such a demeaning way, astral entities will gladly step in and babble some nice sounding words that anyone can find on the Internet. If the entity satisfies the audience, then why not hang around longer and possess some of the weaker ones in the audience. Beware! This one is NOT a Master, but an entity that is violating the rights of free will by trying to trick a whole audience of people.

In general, Masters communicate through your super-conscious mind or soul, not through your ears. This is a surer communication and helps the person distinguish between astral voices and the real hierarchical communications. You receive messages in the form of intuitions or thought-forms through the soul. These messages are likely to be reminders of what is already written in your soul plan rather than to order you to buy this house or go hither and yond.

Moreover messages from the Masters concern the general public, for their love of humanity and commitment to do the will of God, affects all mankind, not just one special person. They do not communicate to advise you on investment strategies, puff up your ego, entertain you with niceties, advise you about your relationship with your spouse, make personal earthly decisions for you, or coddle you because you cannot fulfill your mission.

Communications from the higher levels of the Spiritual Hierarchy have substance. You can read, listen, re-read their messages and each time gain something from them. They are multi-layered and neutral. Rarely are they personally directed, yet the message would apply to your life.

If the Masters begin to communicate with you, it would be at a stage where they (not you) have determined along with your soul that you are reliable and fit enough to carry out your part of the Divine Plan. Their guidance will consist of reminders and suggestions to aid you in carrying out your individual soul plan as it fits into the general Divine Plan for mankind. All must honeycomb together to make the whole.

One misconception floating around the arenas of the New Age movement is that "Do not worry, my dear, you will never be asked to do anything that you are not capable of doing." How nice and comforting but so far from the truth! Let's put it another way. You will be asked to do something that will stretch your every means to accomplish it, and then some. How can the Spiritual Hierarchy test your reliability if the task is always within the bounds of your comfort zone?

Once you have been tried and tested for reliability, the Master can then assign you some very difficult tasks to perform for the Spiritual Hierarchy, all in line with your soul plan. Some could even involve contact with the Dark Forces through clandestine means where your earthly life may be in danger, and this is when the basic question of one's commitment to the mission arises: has your life taken on more importance than the objectives of the Divine Plan which you volunteered to accomplish before this incarnation? This is a tough question and one which all initiates on the Path must eventually encounter. You are left to decide yourself what to do at such a crossroads. No one else can make this determination for you.

Discovering your soul plan will necessarily be a life-changing landmark. The discovery will take place step by step, for as you implement each step, so will you be tried and tested. To be part of so great a scheme as the Divine Plan requires a person who is committed, persistent and reliable. The Spiritual Hierarchy does not compromise on quality even if lightbearers fall by the wayside and the light forces dwindle. The Spiritual Hierarchy will never accept less than the best and if it means waiting until more lightbearers awaken to carry out the plan they promised to do before this incarnation, then will the suffering of the world be prolonged.

The world's karma is coming to a head in conjunction with the end of this sidereal cycle, and ready or not, huge changes will take place. How much pain and suffering humanity undergoes during these changes will depend on if the forces of light come forward as promised.

Epilogue

Mankind's evolution is not directionless. It is pointing toward the Fourth Dimension as part of an intricate long range Divine Plan. In our times, we will only witness the first steps into a new age and dimension, and depending on your individual plan, you may be visiting the onward evolution of this plan with subsequent incarnations, or you will be witnessing it and guiding those who dare to incarnate.

Boundless opportunities beyond our imagination will rise out of the ashes of the present system. The new society will no longer be based on ambition, money, political power, and self-centeredness. All inhabitants will learn to express their soul urgings, and when this happens, the whole of human society reclaim the right evolutionary path. The I AM based society will open up untold abilities and opportunities for each and every inhabitant on earth.

This is the great promise of the New Age which shall unfold after earth cleanses herself. To look beyond the present turmoil and see the great promise that lies beyond should be the prime motivation of all lightbearers who

take up the cross and work diligently to help cleanse and
heal the earth.

4448445

Made in the USA
Charleston, SC
23 January 2010